Braided
Cross Stitch

Braided
Cross Stitch

Art Salemme

Sterling Publishing Co., Inc.   New York

Library of Congress Cataloging-in-Publication Data

Salemme, Art.
  Braided cross stitch.

  Includes index.
  1. Cross-stitch, Long-legged.   I. Title.
TT778.C76S25   1989   746.44   88-36244
ISBN 0-8069-6967-9
ISBN 0-8069-6966-0 (pbk.)

1   3   5   7   9   10   8   6   4   2

Copyright © 1989 by Art Salemme
Published by Sterling Publishing Co., Inc.
Two Park Avenue, New York, N.Y. 10016
Distributed in Canada by Oak Tree Press Ltd.
c/o Canadian Manda Group, P.O. Box 920, Station U
Toronto, Ontario, Canada M8Z 5P9
Distributed in England by Cassell
Artillery House, Artillery Row, London SW1P 1RT, England
Distributed in Australia by Capricorn Ltd.
P.O. Box 665, Lane Cove, NSW 2066
Manufactured in the United States of America
All rights reserved

To Gerry,
who thought that I should be painting
the bedroom;

to Anne, Peter, Jean, John, and Mary,
who thought that I should be writing
that cookbook
I promised them when I retired,
Like Mom and Dad Used To Make;

and to Doris Miller,
who thought that I should be writing
that book on
how to translate scientific-technical
Russian:

Sorry, all, but I got carried away!

▪ Contents ▪

· 1 ·
What *Is* Braided Cross-Stitch?

Tvistsöm is Swedish for a type of braided cross-stitch that has been traditional for centuries in Scandinavia and continues to be popular there. The name is so little known that it seemed wiser to call this book *Braided Cross-Stitch,* which has the merit of being descriptive. Unlike counted cross-stitch, which lies flat on the canvas on which it is worked (Illus. 1), *tvistsöm* forms a raised braid on the canvas (Illus. 2):

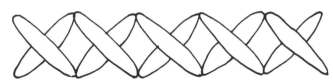

Illus. 1.

Illus. 2. (Note: *In order to show the stitch structure clearly, the sketches of braided cross-stitch in this chapter have a sparser, more "open" appearance than is actually typical of the stitch.)*

Also unlike counted cross-stitch, in which every stitch is made in exactly the same way—first the left-bottom to right-top half of the stitch (Illus. 3), then the right-bottom to left-top half (Illus. 4)—the rows of braided stitches are made

Illus. 3.   *Illus. 4.*

in alternating directions, left and right, thus creating an overall "fabric" in which the two kinds of rows are clearly distinguishable (Illus. 5).

Moreover, if the canvas is turned a quarter-turn before working the alternating rows, the completed piece will also show distinct up-and-down lines in addition to the basic left-and-right ones (Illus. 6).

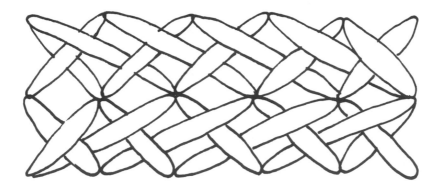

Illus. 5.

The variety of directions possible, combined with the variety of color and texture effects possible, gives the stitch great expressiveness and spontaneity.

Why, then, has the stitch been unfamiliar to so many needleworkers all these years? Is it because of the strangeness of the Swedish name? Although the name *tvistsöm* seems strange to English speakers, the word *söm* is the same word as the English *seam* (and the German *Säume*). Thus, *tvistsöm* really means "twist-seam" or "twist-stitch." But it is never called that in the few English-language needlework books that do refer to it. Instead it is given such names as "long-armed cross-stitch," "long-legged cross-stitch," "plaited Slav stitch," "Arraiolos stitch" (Portuguese rug stitch), etc. As the various names indicate, many countries claim it as their

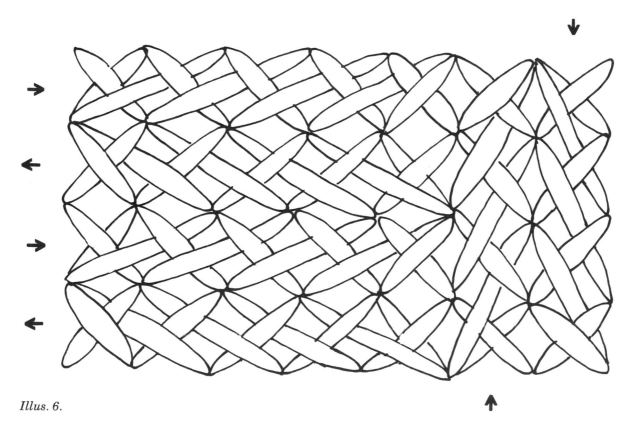

Illus. 6.

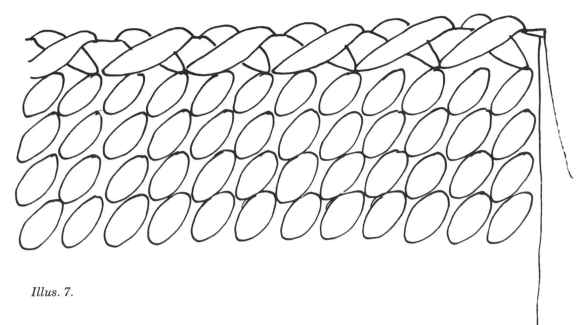

Illus. 7.

own. And yet so many needleworkers, who have eagerly adopted and adapted stitches from virtually every culture, seem to have overlooked this one. Actually, however, the stitch has been known to many, and has indeed been used by them, but not as a decorative stitch. Instead, it is the well-known binding stitch that is used to join pieces of completed needlepoint to another one (Illus. 7).

Well, now it is time to take the binding stitch out of its utilitarian realm and to acquaint needleworkers with its artistic capabilities.

One reason why some needleworkers may have been disinclined to learn to use braided cross-stitch decoratively is that the materials used in Sweden for the stitch are not readily available

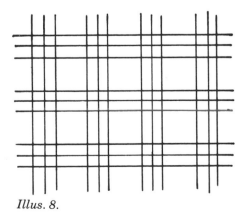

Illus. 8.

elsewhere. In Sweden a special type of canvas is used (very strongly woven triple-thread canvas, 9 holes to the inch)—Illus. 8. Swedish *tvistsöm* yarns are usually two-ply wool. Very often each ply is of a different color, so that the final stitched piece has a "tweedy" look.

My enthusiasm for using this stitch has developed in me a strong desire to popularize it. To fulfill this mission, I have created designs that, I hope, will be recognizable to many: a Maine lighthouse, a New Orleans street, the Golden Gate Bridge on a foggy day. In addition, I have adapted some traditional quilting designs: *Log Cabin, Trip Around the World, Grandmother's Fan,* and so forth. I hope that the designs strike a responsive chord in another reader and make him or her want to recreate the design. Or, better, yet, to create his or her own designs using *tvistsöm*; to reproduce the needleworker's own home, own church, own city or village.

The first step was to simplify things for the needleworker. There is no sense in firing up a person's enthusiasm and then saying, "Now we'll have to order the canvas and yarns from Sweden, which might take eight to ten weeks." So I devised a technique, using easily available canvas and yarns. You can start work this afternoon! All the projects in this book were done on Penelope canvas (double-thread canvas, as distinct from single-thread, or "mono" canvas that is typically used for needlepoint or bargello).

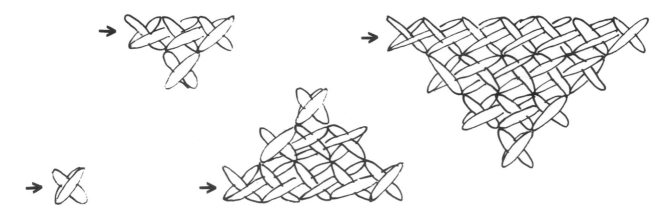

Illus. 9.

Most of the projects were done on canvas that has 6½ pairs of canvas threads per inch (6.5-mesh canvas). To replace the Swedish yarns, I selected three-ply Persian-type, wool needlepoint yarns; separated the yarns into separate plies; then recombined the plies, two at a time, in the needle: Sometimes I used two plies of the same color, but most often I used two plies of different colors, thereby creating the same "tweedy" effect that one gets with the Swedish yarns.

Another reason why some needleworkers may feel that *tvistsöm* is too hard to learn is that both the Swedish instructions and the few English translations state, "Always work the rows left-to-right. When you reach the end of the row, turn canvas upside-down and make the next row left-to-right." In other words a simple triangle executed in this manner (Illus. 9) would have its apex pointing first up, then down, then up, then down, then up, etc. The constant turning of the canvas is confusing, even for an experienced needleworker, not to mention a beginner. Moreover, the instruction "Always work the rows left-to-right" seems to set up an insurmountable obstacle for the left-handed needleworker.

Still another reason why Swedish cross-stitch may not appeal to needleworkers is that the pictorial designs offered do not evoke any senti-

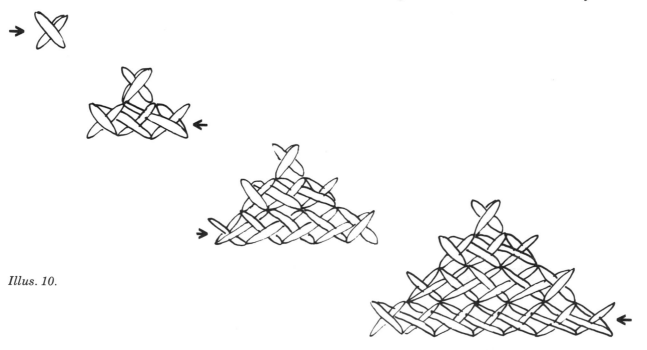

Illus. 10.

mental feelings: they depict Swedish castles or Swedish literary or folklore characters, most of which are unfamiliar to non-Swedes. The non-representational designs often include familiar motifs, universally recognized motifs such as eight-pointed stars and other designs that are very common in Scandinavian knitting and counted cross-stitch. But other nonrepresentational designs that have warm connotations for the Swedish needleworker just don't have the same appeal in other lands.

But most importantly, to make the stitch easier, I developed a way of making the alternating rows of stitches *without* turning the canvas at the end of each row. By this method, the triangle represented in Illus. 9 would look like this as each successive row is made (Illus. 10):

If, when you start working the triangle, you form a mental image of a triangle with one stitch at the apex and nine stitches at the base, you can just keep making the rows until you have the desired triangle, instead of mentally and physically turning that triangle point-up, point-down, point-up, etc. This method also enables a left-handed needleworker to execute the stitch with the same ease as a right-handed one.

· 2 ·
Making a Trial Piece

If you have never done braided cross-stitch before, or if you have done it only by the traditional method, but now would like to switch over to an easier one, you should start with a trial piece. Instead of just a few stitches on a piece of scrap canvas, I think it would be more fun to practise the stitch while also learning how to read the charts as printed in this book. Since the charts are not printed in color, black-and-white symbols have been used to represent the different colors of yarns. Most books on counted cross-stitch and other types of needlework use special symbols to represent colors, but I feel that letter symbols (A, B, C, etc.) are easier to recognize and remember. I have also found that using a single symbol to represent each individual stitch makes it easier to count the stitches than using a single symbol to represent an entire area of several stitches. And finally, I have devised a system of using symbols printed on their side, to represent rows of stitches made vertically.

In the projects presented here, each symbol is equated to a specific color (or blend) of Paternayan three-ply Persian-type wool yarns. But for the trial piece, use whatever three-ply Persian-type yarns you have available, letting each symbol represent a different color (or color blend).

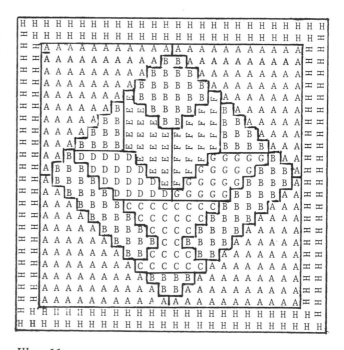

Illus. 11.

14

You could, for example, make the four triangles A in white; basket C in dark brown; background B in medium tan; D, E, F, G in whatever colors you like; and border H in rust (Illus. 11). Or use your own favorite color scheme.

The instructions that follow just provide the facts with relatively few explanations of *why* certain things are recommended. But detailed explanations are available elsewhere in the book, in chapter 5, "Question and Answer Clinic." Therefore, if questions arise in your mind while reading these instructions, such as "Can't I use mono canvas instead of Penelope?" or "Can't I use the zigzag stitch on my sewing machine, instead of masking tape?" refer to that chapter in the book, where I try to answer all conceivable questions.

Supplies needed: 7-inch square of Penelope canvas (double-thread canvas), 6½ pairs of canvas threads per inch ("6.5-mesh")

three-ply Persian-type wool yarn, small quantities —one color (or color blend of two colors) for each symbol in sample diagram

tapestry needle (blunt point) #20.

Prepare canvas: Cut piece of Penelope canvas into 7-inch square. This allows an unworked border of approximately 1½″ all around sample piece. Cover the cut edges of canvas with masking tape.

Prepare yarns: Separate three-ply Persian-type yarns into separate plies. Use two plies in the needle. You may use two plies of the same color, or one ply each of two different colors. Put color A in needle. Do not knot ends.

Find beginning point on canvas: For this trial piece, I recommend that you start with the upper left-hand corner of triangle A—stitch underlined in the chart. Count down ten *rows* of canvas (not ten holes) on left-hand edge of canvas; then count from left to right to tenth set of vertical threads.

Don't forget to count the horizontal rows and the vertical threads that are hidden under the masking tape!

As a beginner, you're allowed to mark the intersection of threads that you have just found. The first stitch will be made over that marked intersection.

Follow the step-by-step diagrams in Illus. 12 to make 11 stitches of color A. Holding canvas in left hand, poke needle up through hole 1 and pull needle through until a "tail" of approximately one inch is left on the back of the canvas. Hold

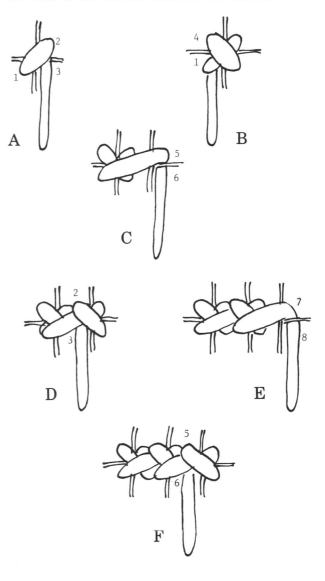

Illus. 12.

15

tail down with fingers of left hand until it is caught tightly by first few stitches. Never make a knot on the back of the canvas.

Now that you have brought the needle and yarn to the front of the canvas, all the stitches are made "like sewing"; that is, insert the point of the needle down into the canvas, then immediately up, and pull the yarn through with a single movement. There is no need to use the time-consuming stab-stitch method that is used for many canvas stitches (poking needle down, pulling yarn all the way through to the back; then poking needle up from the back, and pulling yarn all the way to the top: two movements).

With the needle parallel to the vertical canvas threads, insert your needle at 2, up at 3; pull yarn through. Now return. Insert your needle in at 4, up at 1 again; pull yarn through. This completes a regular cross-stitch. Now forward to the next pair of open holes: Needle in at 5, up at 6; pull yarn through (this makes the "long-armed stitch"); then go back. Your needle in at 2, up at 3; pull yarn through. At this point you have completed your second stitch. Notice that you can count the stitches more easily by counting the canvas threads covered, rather than by counting yarn stitches themselves.

Continue making stitches in this manner, going forward to empty holes for the first half of the stitch, then going back to the preceding pair of holes to complete the stitch. Forward 7-8; back 5-6—three stitches completed. Continue in this manner until 11 stitches of A have been made (that is, until you have completed the stitch that covers the eleventh vertical row of canvas threads, starting with the intersection that you have marked). But you're not finished yet! Whenever you finish a row of stitches, in this instance, 11 stitches of color A, you must complete the row by inserting the needle in the upper corner of the row (see arrow in Illus. 13) and pulling the yarn

through to the back of the canvas. This finishes each row with a regular cross-stitch, just as each row begins with one.

Now practise making a return row on your trial piece. If you were using the traditional method, you would now turn your canvas upside down and possibly get confused. But by using this new method, you do not invert the canvas. Referring to the diagram or to your memory, you realize that you have to make a row of 10 stitches of A directly under the row you have just finished. The row is offset by one stitch on the right side. Find the intersection of canvas threads directly below the next-to-last stitch in the row you have just finished. That intersection will carry the first stitch of your return row of 10 stitches of color A (see arrow in Illus. 14).

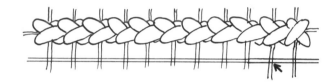

Illus. 14.

Whereas the first row was made moving forward and back, creating a row of stitches from left to right, the return row is made by going forward to empty holes, then going back, creating a row of stitches from right to left. It's easier than it sounds! In Illus. 15 needle up at 1; insert needle in 2, up at 3, pull yarn through. Now go back. Insert your needle in at 4, up at 1 again; pull

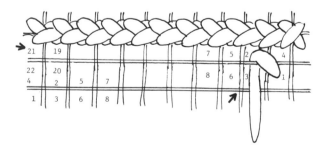

Illus. 15.

Illus 13.

16

yarn through. Forward to 5-6; back to 2-3. Forward 7-8; back 5-6. These stitches are not shown in Illus. 15, but when you get to this point, you have completed three stitches in the reverse row. Continue making stitches until you have gone forward to 21-22, and back to 19-20. That completes the 10 stitches. But, you're still not finished! To finish the row, insert your needle in 21 (arrow at left) and pull yarn to the back, completing the final regular cross-stitch. Second row done!

To make the third row as in the diagram (a row of 9 stitches of color A), locate the intersection directly below the last stitch completed. With that intersection, start the first stitch: Yarn up at 1; needle in at 2, up at 3; pull yarn through. Now continue on your own, stopping after 9 pairs of vertical threads in canvas have been covered (arrow at bottom). Third row done!

Fourth row (8 stitches of color A) is also offset one stitch. Find the appropriate intersection (as with the second row), and make the return row of 8 stitches. Four completed rows shown in Illus. 16. Note that it is easier to count the stitches by the vertical canvas threads that are covered—11 on the first row, 8 on the fourth row—instead of trying to count the braided stitches. Never count the holes!

Somewhere along the line, you may run out of yarn. If you do, you should bring the yarn to the back of the canvas, and run the needle under some completed stitches, then cut the yarn. No knots! Then you should thread the needle with a new supply of yarn (no knot at the end!), run the needle under a different area of completed stitches to fasten the yarn, then bring the needle up to the front of the canvas to continue your work. For more details, see chapter 5, "Question and Answer Clinic."

By this time you have probably noticed a few things. You are not slavishly dependent upon the chart. You do not have to keep referring to it to make this triangle. You can tell yourself mentally, "It's a right triangle, pointing down at the left side, with decreasing rows of 11, 10, 9,...1 stitches." And with that mental image, you can complete the whole triangle before you have to refer to the chart again.

You probably have also noticed that the stitches of one row "share the holes" with the stitches of adjacent rows. Some beginners get confused about this, but the quickest way to get unconfused is to remember that you are covering *intersections* of canvas threads with stitches. Therefore, no intersections should be left uncovered.

And you have also probably noticed that the stitch creates a nice fat braid on the front of the canvas. Only small amounts of yarn appear on the back. With the exception of the starting and ending stitches in each row, the back of the stitches should look like Illus. 17. If any diagonal lines of yarn appear in your work on the backside of the canvas, you weren't holding the needle parallel to the canvas threads. Practise some more.

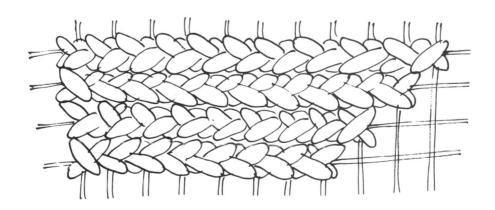

Illus. 16.

Not like this

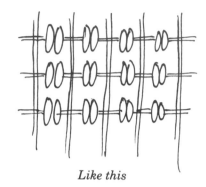

Illus. 17.

Like this

Now continue making that first triangle. Continue until you have completed the row of 2 stitches (a return row). All that remains is to make the very bottom row—a single stitch.

Unlike a regular cross-stitch with two layers of yarn, a braided cross-stitch has *three* layers of yarn to fatten it up to the same height as the rest of the braided stitches. To make a single stitch (Illus. 18), bring yarn up at 1. Needle in at 2, up at 3; pull yarn through. Then needle in at 4, up at 1 again; pull yarn through. This completes what would ordinarily be a regular cross-stitch,

but, as with any row of braided cross-stitches, you have to insert the needle in the upper corner and pull the yarn to the back of the canvas. When you do that with a single stitch, that lays the third layer of yarn on top to make it the right height.

Now that you have completed one triangle of color A, why not try another color? Take color B of your choice (separate three-ply Persian of one or two colors; then put two plies of your choice in the needle), and work the diamond (or "square on point," to use a quilter's term) that fits under the four top rows of the triangle you just finished. Looking at the chart, you see that you will make rows of 2 stitches, then 4, then 6, then 6-4-2 again. That's easy to remember and to do. But a very slight problem! It is a problem that one always encounters when starting an area of new color. "Do you start with a regular row of stitches, or a return row?" As you become more proficient, you will be able to recognize the two kinds of rows. But for now, I'll remind you that the row of "B B" at the top of the diamond is right next to the second row of A that you worked, which was a return row. Therefore, you should make the "B B" row also as a return row (Illus. 19) and then continue alternating the row directions as you did with the triangle. Numbers 1-2-3-4 in Illus. 19 indicate location of first stitch in that return row.

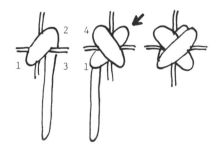

Illus. 18.

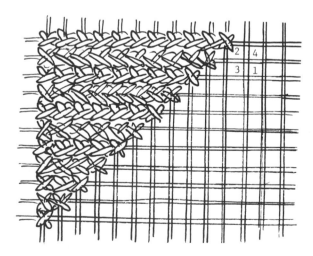

Illus. 19.

Continue working areas of A, B, C, D. Then do G. That leaves areas E, F, and H unworked. Areas E and F have their letter-symbols printed on the side. Areas of H (the border) have two sides of the "frame" with letter-symbols printed on the side, and two sides with regular letter-symbols. To make stitches with symbols printed on the side, turn the chart one-quarter turn clockwise (I hope you younger readers with digital watches know what I mean) until the letters read right. Then turn your canvas a quarter-turn clockwise to conform to the chart.

With the chart in the turned position, count down to first row of "E E E E E." It is row 10 (even number). Hence it is a return row. Start the first stitch of E at arrow (Illus. 20). Do that row, then alternate three more rows of E. Then four rows of F.

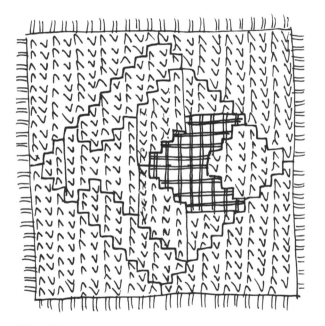

Illus. 20.

Now do the frame, in color H. You might have asked yourself, way back at the beginning, "Why didn't I just start at the very top of the diagram, with the first row of color H?" The answer is that when a beginner does the frame first, and then works the stitches closer and closer to the center, like the center of a whirlpool, he or she often finds that the unworked canvas in the center is either one square too big or one square too small on each side. The needleworker had miscounted the number of stitches in the very first row! He or she made, say, 27 stitches, rather than the 26 stitches required. To prevent tragedies such as this, it is always safer to work the frame last, making stitches "round and round" without even bothering to count the stitches. Just keep a-stitchin' until you encircle the piece, and then the number of stitches *has* to be right.

In this trial piece, since the innermost row of H is row 2 (even number) from the top, it is a return row. Make a return row of H next to the top row of the completed top triangles of A. Turn canvas one-quarter turn, and continue making a return row of H down the left-hand side of design. Turn canvas another quarter-turn and make third side of innermost border row. Turn again, and complete fourth side. This completes the innermost row of frame H.

Now do the outermost row of frame H. Make a regular row H; a quarter-turn of canvas counterclockwise and continue stitching; quarter-turn again for the third side; quarter-turn again for the fourth side. Piece finished!

Now that you have finished the sample piece in your favorite colors, aren't you proud of yourself? Doesn't it look pretty? Don't you like the effect of the horizontal rows of stitching, with the occasional accents of areas with the stitching going up and down and the mitred effect where you made the border? Don't you like the perfect squareness of the finished piece? Braided cross-stitch does not pull the canvas out of shape, the way some canvas stitches do. It is self-correcting: the first half of each stitch pulls in one direction and the second half pulls in the opposite direction, thus remaining perfectly square as you go.

Finally, didn't you find it fun to see the design grow by following the chart and choosing your own colors to represent the various letter-symbols?

All of the projects in this book can be reproduced by using the stitch and technique you have just mastered. The stitch itself is simple, but the beauty of any of the designs results from the blendings of colors and the directions of the rows of stitches. I hope that you will get as much pleasure out of making the pieces as I did in designing and working them. But, most of all, I hope that you will eventually want to design and execute your own pieces. Accordingly, I have given, in another chapter of this book, complete directions for converting your favorite design or favorite scene, whether hastily sketched, on a postcard or photograph, or whatever, to this very versatile, very expressive kind of needlework. Quick, run out and show your friends and relatives the beautiful piece of braided cross-stitch you just completed, and then teach them how to do it too. Spread the word!

· 3 ·
Projects

To get the inspiration for the projects in this book, I looked around and asked myself what appeals to me. I hoped that, if I was interested in certain motifs such as quilt designs and in scenes suggested by my own environment and travels, then those designs and scenes would also appeal to other needleworkers. The familiarity of the design elements would take away some of the "foreignness" of the stitch and encourage new needleworkers to give braided cross-stitch the place it deserves.

Many of the designs in this book were inspired by traditional quilts—*Log Cabin, Trip Around the World, Double Irish Chain,* etc. Others were inspired by real or fanciful situations incorporating a quilt. Still others were inspired by American scenes that are familiar to most—the Mall in Washington, D. C., a Maine lighthouse, a New Orleans street.

The design ideas came rushing into my head from anywhere and everywhere. Every devoted needleworker knows the sensation: You are working on one project, but are already mentally planning the next project. And the one after that. And even before you can start them, you have thought of still more ideas that you want to get

to. In preparing this book, I limited myself to 25 designs, but I could have easily executed hundreds of designs from everywhere. There is inspiration in hundreds and thousands of traditional and contemporary quilt designs, from traditional weaving designs, from cross-stitch designs, from American Indian rug-weaving and basketmaking motifs.

With the space limitations of this book, I have not included several projects that I completed and that may be just the thing you are looking for. Maybe you'll see them in my next book! Or maybe you yourself will get impatient and decide to "do it yourself." It's easy to do! Look around you and see what makes you feel nice. Is it your cat sitting on the windowsill, under your favorite spider plant in the macramé hanger that your daughter made for you before she got married and moved so far away? Why not reproduce that scene? Stitch "Mister Kat" in variegated shades of orange and cream. Stitch the macramé hanger with its big brown wooden beads. Stitch the spider plant in juicy greens that suggest the bright sunlight in the window. When you're finished, send it to your daughter.

Just as all the designs in this book are the result of my own experience, they were all executed by me. Not only did I have the fun of designing them, but also the excitement of transforming a germ of an idea into pleasing colors and forms. Put in a tree against the sky! What color leaves should it have? How bright should the blue sky be? Those were questions that I had to resolve as I was executing the designs. And it often happened that the colors that I had originally visualized proved incorrect. Then I would have to take out that "perfect blue" in that entire carefully worked area and put in what I had thought would be too bland a blue, and now the effect *was* perfect! The tree stood out in sharp relief!

Because I was designing as I went, I could not rely on a phalanx of "devoted friends and students" to execute the pieces for this book. Therefore, I cannot express my appreciation to 25 needleworkers from Anna May Ambercrombie to Zelda Zimmerman (I don't know anyone whose last name begins with an X) for having "done the stitchery." One close friend of mine—Alice Skarda, past president of The National Quilting Association, and currently the president of the Prince George's Historical Quilting Society— asked me several times if she and some of her friends couldn't help me by executing some of the designs for this book. They would act as guinea pigs to double-check the charts and instructions. But I had to assure Alice that I wouldn't have any charts until the piece was done.

"But," Alice would say, "there must be some designs, like *Trip Around the World,* in which once you have selected the colors, someone else could actually do the hours and hours of stitching." No, I wanted to execute even those designs by myself. It would be unfair to expect anyone else to do hours of what he or she might consider to be repetitive, noncreative work or drudgery. As the designer, I did not and do not consider it drudgery to do large areas of monotonous stitching—for example, several rows of a single color encircling or framing a completed picture. It is while doing those repetitive, almost automatic actions that the needleworker is able to let his or her mind go free: not just to think about ideas for future projects, but also to think peacefully about "things in general." I couldn't ask Alice or anyone else to stitch hundreds of *my* stitches in anything even slightly resembling a stressful

situation: "I told Art I'd have this piece finished by today, but I just can't get excited about doing that tremendous border."

And, finally, what if I had actually asked someone else to do the *Navajo Rug Design,* the *Cathedral Window,* the *Hawaiian Breadfruit Appliqué,* or any of the other designs that came out nicely, but which I decided not to include in this book? I don't think I could be brave enough to say, "Thanks a lot for doing the piece, but I've decided not to put it in the book."

What, then, was my modus operandi after deriving inspiration from whatever source? First I decided what I wanted. Then I decided on the size. Then I charted the design tentatively on graph paper. Cutting a piece of canvas large enough to accommodate the design, I selected colors of Persian yarns from my "palette" of three-ply yarns. Then I worked from the tentative chart, making any desirable color or design adjustments. *Instead of making the basket in the same color of brown throughout, why not use two different colors, with the rows of* tvistsöm *running one way for one color and running another way for the second color?* As I made color or design adjustments in the tentative chart, I recorded any changes, changing the outside border, for example, from three rows to four rows, and also recording the order numbers of the Persian yarns actually used in the final composition. Once the piece was completed, I drew a final chart, using a system of symbols to key the various colors (or color blends) to the appropriate order numbers of the Persian yarns.

In assigning the symbols I attempted to provide some kind of mnemonic assistance to the needleworker so that, by looking at the symbol, he or she could instantaneously convert that symbol mentally to a yarn color, instead of having to refer to a list showing, for example, that + stands for color 261. Unfortunately, because of the variations among the designs themselves— some of which are nonrepresentational with a relatively small number of colors, and others of which are pictorial with a rather large number of color variations—it was not possible to use a system of symbols that is consistent throughout the entire book. It was not possible, for example, to use the system that is used in some cross-stitch books, in which the symbol ‡ always stands for

22

"color 246, medium blue-green." In this book I have few arbitrary symbols (symbol – stands for "white, 260" in one design, but for "dark purple, 310" in another design). Whenever possible, however, I have used a mnemonic system in which, for example, Y stands for "yellow," O stands for "orange," W for "white," and so forth. Or, if not for colors, the symbols stand for pictorial elements: W stands for "water," B stands for "bridge," and so forth.

But in many designs the mnemonic system falls by the wayside: A, B, C represent different colors in the sky, or in a traditional quilt design, A, B, C represent completely different colors of geometric shapes. But don't fret! As you work each design, you will find it easy to remember that in the design you are working, A is the blue-and-white blend, B is the light blue, and C is the medium blue. Remember also that, as Emerson said, "A foolish consistency is the hobgoblin of little minds." At any rate, I have indicated the less obvious mnemonics for you: O is "olive green," D is "dark green."

The numbers equated to the symbols represent the order numbers of Paternayan "Paterna Persian Yarn, 100% virgin wool," a three-ply needlework yarn that is available in most places. Some yarn shops sell it by the single strand when only a small quantity is required. Other shops sell it by 8-yard skeins. And some mail-order needlework supply houses sell it by 8-yard or 40-yard skeins. Because of the large number of variables —your choice of canvas with 6, 6½, or 7 holes per inch, the tightness or looseness with which you personally make the stitch, the length of yarn strands that your local yarn shop sells or the length that you cut to work with, the amount of waste that you have when beginning and ending each group of stitches in a particular color, etc.— I have not indicated the quantities of yarn required for each piece. In some designs it is obvious that only an infinitesimal amount of one color is needed—for example, the one stitch of bright blue in *Maine Lighthouse* to represent the starry field of the American flag. In other designs a large amount of wool of a certain color will be needed to complete the border. I advise the "trial and error" method. Order more than you think you will need, but make arrangements with the yarn shop owner that you can return the unused,

uncut skeins, accompanied by the sales receipt, and obtain a refund or exchange. But I'll predict that you will hang onto any overestimated quantities of Persian yarns and use them in future braided cross-stitch projects.

This is exactly the same situation as encountered by quiltmakers, who have to estimate how much fabric to order. "The instructions say to buy a yard, but I'd better buy an extra yard to allow for mistakes or changes. While I'm at it, I'll get an extra yard because it's on sale, and two more extra yards because I really love the color!" That's the way that quilters get those wonderful collections of fabrics that they catalogue and store so carefully until they want to use them. By the time they get around to using that "perfectly pink" fabric with the tiny flowers, they have forgotten how much it cost. Let's hope that you too can build up a collection of Persian yarns from your miscalculations, so that, when you get around to using them, you can say, even though you know otherwise, "They didn't cost me a penny!—they're leftovers."

For each piece in this book I have indicated the kind of canvas used, the size to cut it (allowing for an unworked border all around), the number of stitches from left to right and the number of rows from top to bottom, and the completed size of the finished piece. If you decide to use a different kind of canvas (using, for example, canvas that has 6 mesh to the inch instead of the 6½ to the inch as used in the original design), the number of stitches will remain the same, but the size of the canvas that you cut will have to be changed. In all instances, when changing the canvas size, count the number of mesh (canvas thread intersections) *very carefully* to make sure that you are allowing enough canvas for the number of stitches and rows required. Then allow, on top and bottom and sides of the canvas, enough canvas for an unworked 1½" border of canvas all around. Then cut! Better yet, you might want to follow the advice of a Russian proverb, "Measure seven times, cut once." There is nothing worse than cutting a piece of canvas to a size that you think is more than adequate, and then finding, after you have put a lot of work into it, that you're going to be ½" short at the bottom. Warning: Some canvas manufacturers are undependable. Some canvas that is supposed to have the same number of mesh in both directions actually proves to be slightly off. On "6-mesh canvas," for example, 60 stitches may measure 10″ in one direction, but 9½″ or 10½″ in the other direction. This usually does not make any appreciable difference in the final appearance of the completed work, but it must be taken into consideration before cutting the canvas before use. So make sure you count the intersections; do not just count the number of inches on a ruler, before you cut the canvas and begin any of the projects in this book.

Some of the designs have small amounts of simple embroidery added to them after the project is completed. The embroidery stitches—backstitch and straight stitch—and a recommended hand-sewn finishing stitch are described in chapter 5, "Question and Answer Clinic."

Let's see now. Did I tell you everything you need to know to get started? I've told you, in chapter 2, how to do the stitch itself. And in this chapter I've told you how to interpret each symbol in the chart and convert it to two plies of three-ply Paternayan yarn that has been separated into three individual plies and then recombined, putting two individual plies in the needle—either two plies of the same color, as in the designation "260/260," or one ply each of two different colors, as in the designation "212/342." But one more reminder: When the letter symbols are printed like normal letters, the rows of stitches that they represent are made with the canvas held in the normal position. But when the letter symbols are printed on their side, it is necessary first to turn the diagram to make the letters "read right," and then to turn the canvas correspondingly before making the stitches.

No attempt has been made to group the projects that follow in order of increasing complexity. But it should be fairly obvious that the charts that look simple (for example, those that have large areas of the same color symbol) are actually simpler to execute than those that *look* complicated (those having areas with many changes of color). But, it is often the "more complicated" designs in any kind of needlework that keep the needleworker engrossed for hours and hours at a time. So don't be afraid to try the projects that "look hard." Remember that the entire project uses only one basic stitch, and any complexity results only from the changing of colors and directions.

A small note about the charts in relationship to the photographs in the book: The charts represent each and every stitch that I put into the design. When I took the pieces to a professional picture-framer to be put in mats and frames, he said that he would make the mats cover one row of stitches all around, to ensure that no canvas would be visible along the edges. "No!" I told him, "each and every stitch has to show, so that the charts will correspond exactly to the photographs!" He said that he would do it my way. But I have decided that professional picture-framers are like our dog Oliver: you tell Oliver repeatedly that you don't want him on the bed, he *knows* that he's not supposed to jump up on the bed, and yet.... So I'm afraid that some of the photographs are at variance with the charts because the mats in the picture frames cover over a few stitches on the top, sides, or bottom. I guess the picture-framer, like Oliver, "sort of forgot" what he wasn't supposed to do.

But certainly you must be ready now, after this lengthy introduction, to jump right in and start making your first braided cross-stitch piece from this book. So I'll get out of your way and let you get started.

1: *Grandmother's Fan* Fan

Shown in color on page C of the color section.

This scene is completely imaginary, but it is typical of quilt shows, where a viewer's attire and accessories often proclaim her favorite quilting medium and echo the quilt that she is studying so intently and that will definitely receive her "Viewer's Choice" ballot. Although the scene is theoretically one that never existed in real life, some of the members of our weekly quilting group insist, "That's got to be Virginia!"

Others insist, just as strenuously, "No, it's got to be Alice!" The people in the latter contingent point out that the quilt is "definitely Alice's colors!" and the quilt rack is like the one that Alice's husband, Don, made for a quilt show several years ago. And yet, Alice doesn't have hair that color, or a jacket or tote bag with *Grandmother's Fan* on it...

I think that a lot of the fun with braided cross-stitch, as with any form of graphic expression, is the freedom with which one can make own's own reality. If you are drawing a scene or rendering it in yarn, and a tree is in the way, move it! If you are doing a picture of your house, put the flowering dogwood tree back in the scene, even though it has been years since it died. Create your scenes the way a novelist creates his characters: One person's physical attributes, another person's occupational habits, a third person's speech patterns. So I really can't say *who "Grandmother's Fan"* Fan is. But I've seen her at quilt shows many times!

CANVAS

Penelope, 6½ pairs of canvas threads per inch (6.5-mesh); cut 12 × 14 inches.

NUMBER OF STITCHES AND ROWS

56 × 74 (size of finished work: 8½ × 11½ inches).

COLOR SCHEME

	Grandmother's Fan quilt	
–	white	260/260
a	medium purple	302/302
b	bright fuchsia	350/350
c	medium orchid	322/322
d	pinkish purple	353/353
e	purple	332/332
f	pale purple	304/304
	Rack	
y	dark brown	461/461
z	medium brown	424/424

Color scheme continued on page 26; chart on page 27.

Nine-Patch quilt (assorted blues):

1	585/585
2	580/580
3	571/571
4	583/583
5	546/546
6	501/501
7	545/545
8	561/561
9	563/563
0	521/521
@	552/552

Triangles quilt

=	924/924
1	585/585
4	583/583
7	545/545
$	932/932

Quilt fan

h	hair	two greys	211/212
j	jacket	copen	503/503
s	skirt	light blue	505/505

Fan on jacket and tote:

k	580/580
7	545/545
m	594/594
n	591/591
p	661/661

Blue ribbon

r	544/544
7	545/545

Wall

−	light grey	204/204

Floor

+	dark tan	435/435

Illus. 21. On facing page: Chart for "Grandmother's Fan" Fan.

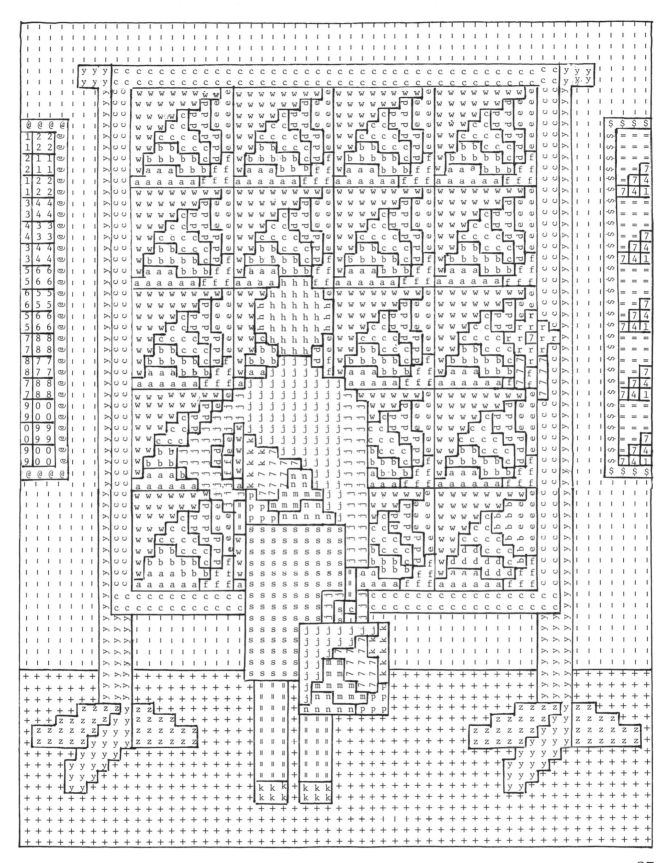

27

2: Bar Harbor

Shown in color on page G of the color section.

Design is based on a sketch that I made in Bar Harbor, Maine, several years ago. While converting the sketch to braided cross-stitch, I wondered whether my watercolor shorthand and my recollection were accurate enough. In August 1985 my wife and I went on a tour of Nova Scotia and contiguous regions. As we swung through Maine, I was able to verify that many of the colors are correct. Those that aren't are probably buildings that were repainted in the interim—certainly my recollection couldn't have been faulty!

CANVAS

Penelope canvas, 6½ pairs of canvas threads per inch ("6.5-mesh"); cut 11 × 11 inches.

NUMBER OF STITCHES AND ROWS

56 × 56 (size of finished work: 8½ × 8½ inches).

COLOR SCHEME

Houses

B	light grey	256/256
J	medium grey	212/212
K	blue-green	521/521
L	orange/red	862/932
O	brown/red	870/930
P	medium-dark grey	211/211
Q	brick red	851/851
R	bright red	970/970

Cars

A	light & teal blue	503/546
C	dark grey/black	210/220
S	medium bright blue	552/552
T	dark bright blue	541/541
Y	bright yellow	712/712
g	teal blue	503/503

Lamp Posts

M	dark grey	210/210
N	black	220/220

Sky

a	white & light blue	260/546
b	light blue	546/546
c	light aqua	585/585

Water

d	white	260/260
e	medium blue	544/544
f	medium-light blue	554/554

Trees

D	orange brown	870/870
U	dark brown	470/470
V	reddish brown	402/402
E	dark green	690/690
f	dark blue green	661/661
G	bright green	620/620
H	dark olive green	650/650
I	dark forest green	601/601

Hills

h	dark yellow-green	692/692
i	medium yellow-green	693/693

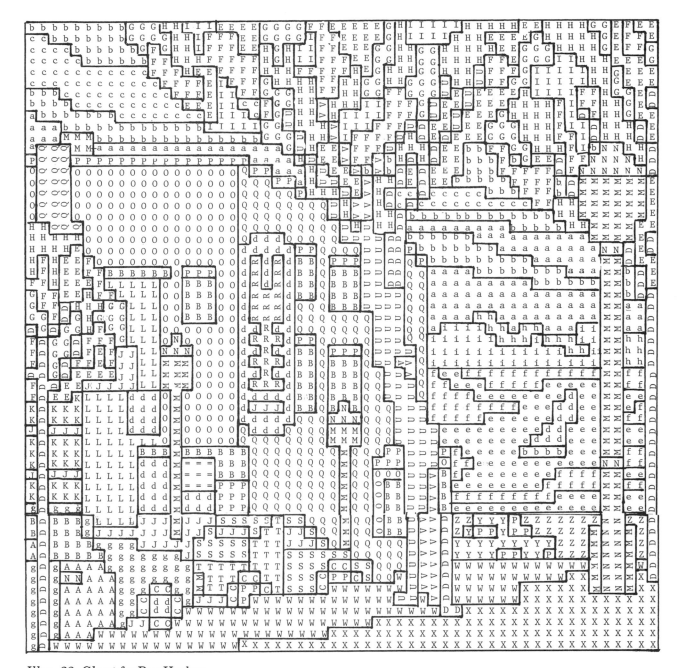

Illus. 22. Chart for Bar Harbor.

Color scheme (cont.)				*Other*

Grass and sidewalks

W	yellow-greens	692/693
X	grey & tan	212/445
Z	pearl grey	204/204

Other

= braided cross-stitch in white (260/260), then embroidered: half cross-stitch with one strand of red (970). (Make half cross-stitch like first stroke of a capital V: \\)

3: Beach House

Shown in color on page H of the color section.

For many years a house in our neighborhood has intrigued me. Its architecture is, in its way, as distinctive as that of the Octagon House in Washington, D. C., or Monticello. When I started doing the pieces for this book, I knew that I would have to include this house. After sketching it and converting the sketch to a grid, I began working the stitches. Before long, a luminous quality began to emerge from the scene. It seemed to me that the house belonged on a beach. I could see people in bathing suits tracking sand through all the oddly shaped rooms, and visualized two or three sets of teen-aged cousins sharing the large room under the pyramidal roof. So I "moved the house to the beach," plunked it on the sand, added a few of the day lilies that I always see around beach houses, and the people who own it don't know the difference.

CANVAS
Penelope canvas, 6½ pairs of canvas threads per inch ("6.5-mesh"); cut 10 × 13 inches.

NUMBER OF STITCHES AND ROWS
71 × 48 (size of finished work: approximately 12 × 8 inches).

COLOR SCHEME

House

L	*light* grey	203/256
M	*medium* grey	211/212
D	*dark* grey	210/210
b	*black*	220/220
–	cream	261/261
T	light blues (*trim*)	546/554
Y	dark red	930/930
Z	darker red	900/900

Sky (four light blues)

a	546/546
b	515/515
c	505/505
d	554/554

Ocean (four medium blues)

e	503/503
f	521/521
h	543/543
i	541/541

Grass and day lilies

g	light & med. chartreuse	670/692
o	orange	833/833
j	medium chartreuse	692/692
k	light chartreuse	670/670

Sand (three tans)

1	414/414
2	435/435
3	490/490

Embroidery
After braided cross-stitch is completed, divide each window into four separate panes by using one ply of blue 554: one long vertical straight stitch to divide area of cream (261) into two equal vertical sections; then one long horizontal straight stitch across middle of vertical straight stitch. (Windows that are only one stitch wide have only the horizontal straight stitch embroidered in blue.)

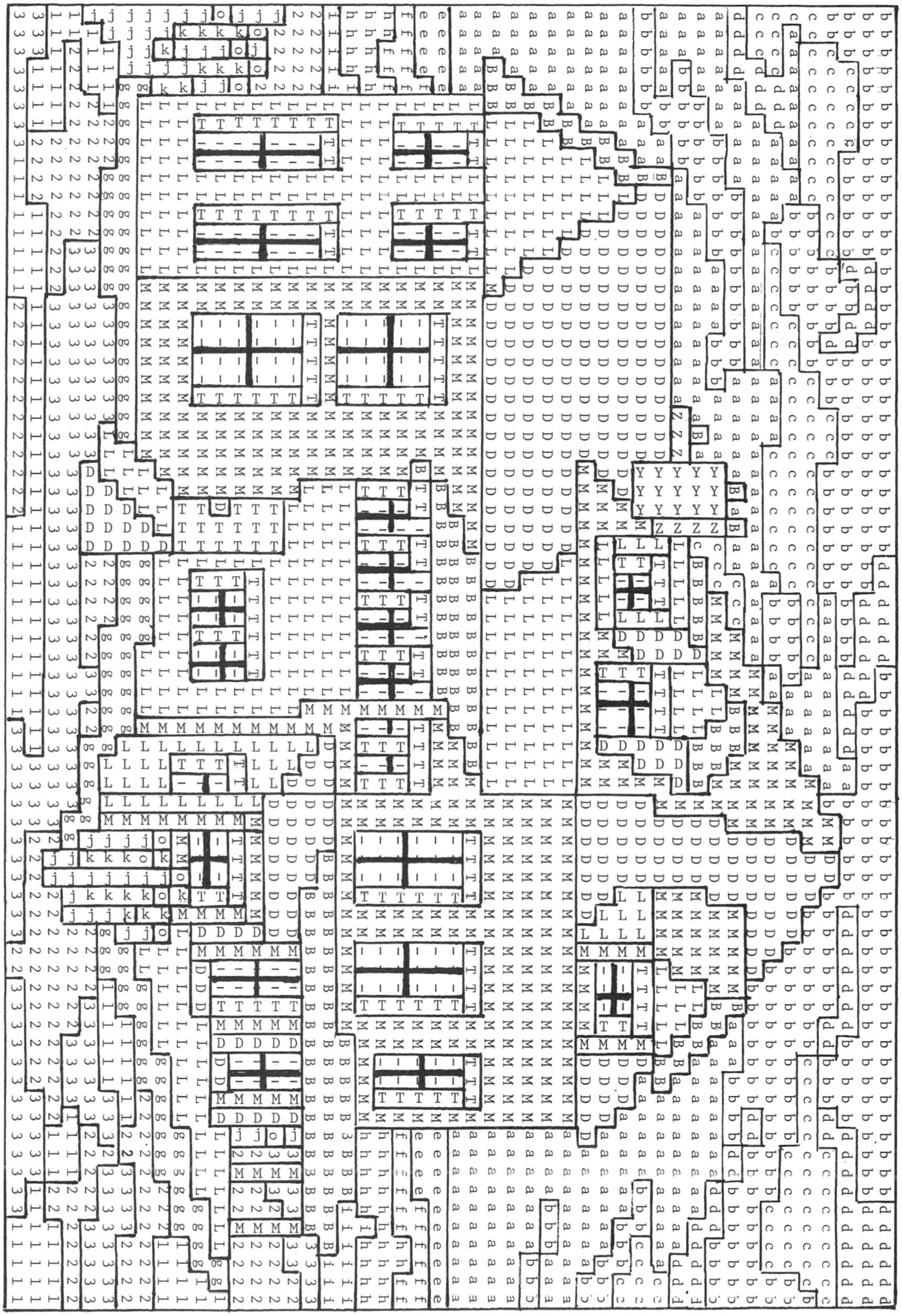

Illus. 23. Chart for Beach House.

4: Cat Mola

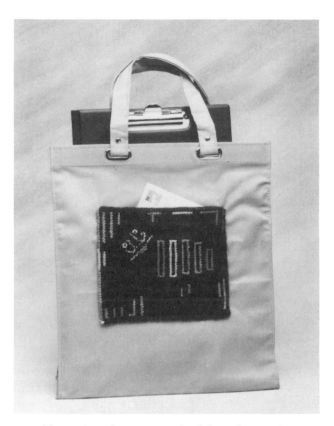

Shown in color on page A of the color section.

If you can't find a real made-by-a-Cuna-Indian mola in your area, or if you have read a book on how to do it, have tried it, and are now convinced that it's really pretty tough to do, you might want to make this "fake mola" in braided cross-stitch. I assure you that you can finish it in much quicker time than you can master the art of mola-making in fabric.

After I finished the *Cat Mola*, I made it into a pocket for a purchased tote (see *Q&A 38*).

CANVAS
Penelope canvas, 6½ pairs of canvas threads per inch ("6.5-mesh"); cut 10 × 11 inches.

NUMBER OF STITCHES AND ROWS
52 × 45 (size of finished work: 8½ × 7½ inches).

COLOR SCHEME

–	red	940/940
X	black	220/220
O	*o*range	811/811
C	*c*hartreuse	670/670
Y	*y*ellow	771/771
L	*l*ilac	302/302
A	*a*pple green	621/621
P	*p*ink	943/943
G	green	696/696
T	*t*an	474/474

Embroidery (backstitches):

nose	302
whiskers	771
around eyes	260 (white)

The *mola* is a distinctive form of stitchery that presumably originated with the Cuna Indians who inhabit the San Blas Islands off the coast of Panama. Some describe the form as "reverse appliqué." At any rate, if you go to Panama you can see hundreds and thousands of molas, and, if you're anything like me, you'll want to buy each one! Some are based on geometric motifs (some claim that these motifs are vestiges of the body-painting the Cunas used to engage in). Many molas are based on whatever local scenes, including local billboards and TV ads, appeal to the mola-maker.

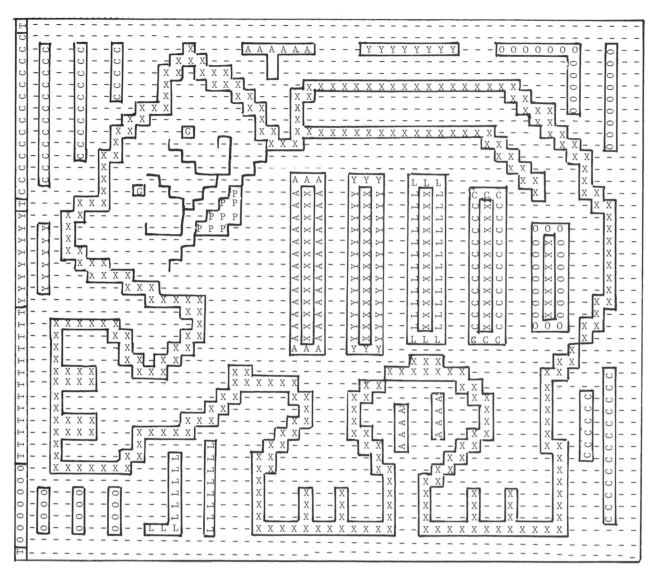

Illus. 24. Chart for Cat Mola.

5: Cat on TV

Shown in color on page A of the color section.

CANVAS

Penelope canvas, 6½ pairs of canvas threads per inch (6.5-mesh); cut 12 × 12 inches.

NUMBER OF STITCHES AND ROWS

58 × 59 (size of finished work: 9 × 9¼ inches).

COLOR SCHEME

Cat

b	grey & *brown*	210/461
o	tan & *orange-tan*	445/885
g	light *grey*	213/213
w	*white*	261/261
x	purplish pink	354/354

TV

g	light *grey*	213/213
G	dark *grey*	201/201
N	*navy* blue	571/571

TV screen

h	two yellows (*hair*)	713/770
.	pink	946/946
1	light chartreuse	653/653
2	medium green	632/632
3	medium olive	651/651
4	dark forest green	610/610
5	light green	634/634
w	*white*	261/261
—	medium tan	436/436

Table & Wall

t	orange-brown	481/481
T	dark brown	461/461
=	light tan	445/445

Embroidery

Cat's features: backstitch with one ply of dark brown (461). Cat's whiskers—3 on each cheek (not shown in chart): straight stitches in ordinary white sewing thread.

TV antenna: Embroidery floss, dark grey (DMC No. 414), 6-strand: one long straight stitch for each antenna. Finish off the end of each antenna with a small black bead.

Our cat Skinny (the name used to be appropriate) has always loved to sleep on top of our small television set. It seemed that, even as he slept, he knew exactly when to hang his tail right down in front of what we were looking at. This scene shows Skinny enhancing a television series on quilting.

Lately there haven't been as many quilting series on television as previously. Also, Skinny has not been up on top of the TV set as frequently. He had some mysterious accident last year that cut down his supply of lives (which had already been reduced from nine to about one and a half) to "running on empty." Although he has recovered from the accident and the surgery (including various pins and wires) to repair his right hind leg, he just can't seem to get any good jumping distance back. How I wish there were another TV series for quilters on the air again, and Skinny could jump up on top of the TV again, to enjoy the show in his own way.

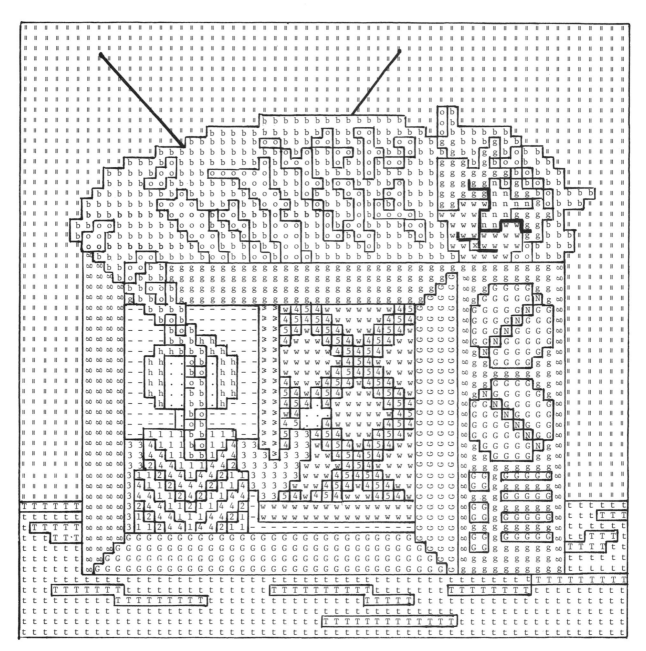

Illus. 25. Chart for Cat on TV.

6: Double Irish Chain

Shown in color on page D of the color section.

A traditional quilt design. Many purists insist that the only "correct" colors for an *Irish Chain* quilt are green and white, but there are many people, even in Ireland, who disagree. This version is made in colors that are suggested by the Amish quilt palette.

CANVAS

Penelope canvas, 6½ pairs of canvas threads per inch ("6.5-mesh"); cut 14 × 14 inches.

NUMBER OF ROWS AND STITCHES

74 × 74 (size of finished work: 11 × 11 inches).

COLOR SCHEME

–	dark purple	310/310
o	light blue-green	591/591
+	medium green	690/690

Illus. 26. Chart for Double Irish Chain, *continued on facing page.*

7: English Sheep

Shown in color on page F of the color section.

CANVAS

Penelope canvas, 6½ pairs of canvas thread per inch (6.5-mesh); cut 10 × 10 inches.

NUMBER OF STITCHES AND ROWS

46 × 40 (size of finished work: 7⅝ × 6⅝ inches).

COLOR SCHEME

Sheep

w	*w*hite	260/715
g	light *g*rey	202/203
G	dark *g*rey	201/210
B	*b*lack	220/220
s	brown	481/900
E	brown (*e*ye)	900/900

Ground

y	*y*ellow	754/754
t	yellow/*t*an	704/745
T	*t*an	435/435
L	*l*ight green	670/704
R	g*r*ey green	693/693
C	*c*hartreuse	670/670
N	bright gree*n*	670/692
M	*m*edium green	690/692
O	*o*live green	650/650
D	*d*ark green	610/610

Embroidery

After piece is worked, backstitch with 1 ply of black (220): eyebrows and Y-shaped nose and philtrum (only philtrum is indicated on chart).

While our friends Jinny and Don Sittler were vacationing in the Lake District in England, they saw a sheep waiting to be photographed. Jinny sent me a copy of the photograph, labelling it "Rya rug on the hoof." I got the idea of rendering the sheep in braided cross-stitch and giving it to Jinny and Don as a memento of their trip. The result was so successful that it started the creative urge and, indeed, prompted me to write this book.

When I first saw the photograph and tried to reproduce faithfully the two spots of reddish-brown wool on the sheep's back, I thought that I was dealing with an identifying color code that the sheep's owner had put on it. I have since been told that it is not the sheep's owner that applies the dye, but rather...well, it's a way by which the flock bloodlines can be recorded accurately.

Illus. 27. On facing page: Chart for English Sheep.

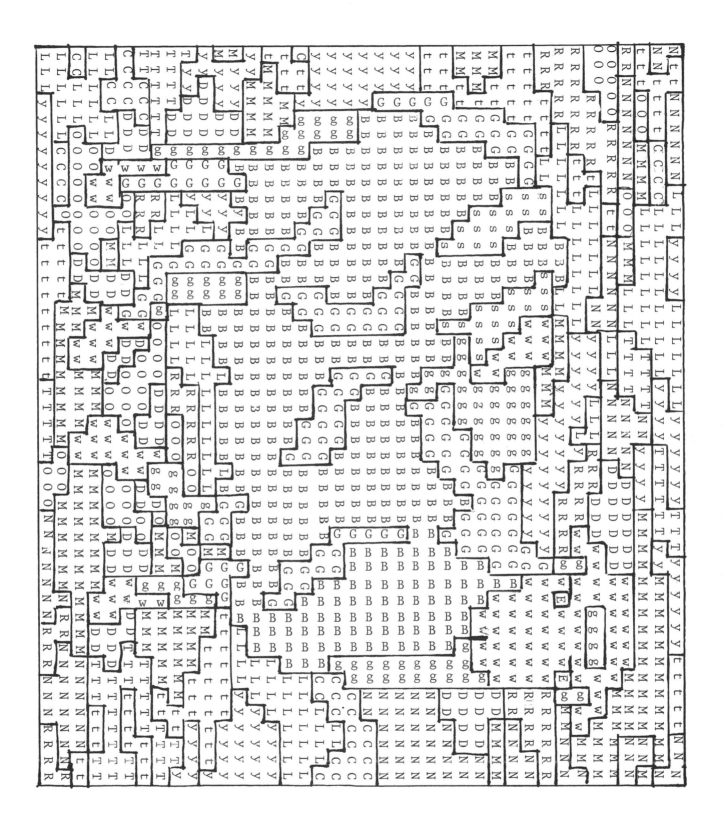

39

8: Four Birds

Shown in color on page E of the color section.

CANVAS

Penelope canvas, 6½ pairs of canvas threads per inch (6.5-mesh); cut 13 × 13 inches.

NUMBER OF STITCHES AND ROWS

68 × 68 (size of finished work: 10 × 10 inches).

COLOR SCHEME

Sea gull

Sky

a	545/545

Bird

b	220/220
c	260/260
d	202/204
e	210/210
$	930/930
f	751/751

Beach

g	621/698
h	445/445
i	436/436

Water

j	541/541
k	501/541
m	501/501
n	501/583
o	583/583
p	583/591
q	591/591

Braided cross-stitch enables the needleworker to derive inspiration from anywhere, and to recycle one's favorite motifs. In this piece, the sea gull could be called a third-generation motif. It started life as a photograph of a sea gull in an advertisement intended to lure me into buying some ocean-front property. It didn't work, but I adapted the photograph a few years ago to the strip-quilting technique of making patchwork pictures and made a 12″ patchwork block based the sea gull. I adapted the design of the patch-work block in order to give the sea gull his third life in braided cross-stitch.

The Canada goose is based on a photograph in a bird book; the mallard reproduces a small carving we bought on vacation in duck country years ago; and the Fulmar petrel is based on one of four hand-colored plates from an Audubon book that have been framed and hanging on our wall for more than a quarter of a century.

Mallard

Sky
r	515/585
s	204/585

Reeds
t	611/611
u	461/461

Bird
v	610/662
c	260/260
#	702/702
w	202/202
x	461/461
j	541/541
b	220/220
A	261/261

Water
p	583/591
y	501/502
z	202/583

Embroidery:

Five backstitches in 501 at bottom of wing.

Canada Goose

Sky
B	204/204
C	204/506
D	506/506
E	506/545
a	545/545

Bird
F	203/203
G	474/474
H	745/745
J	470/470
K	441/441
L	403/403
M	435/435
b	220/220
c	260/260
e	210/210
w	202/202

Fulmar Petrel

Sky
N	212/212
P	202/212
Q	202/203
w	202/202

Water
R	501/501
S	502/502

Rocks
T	210/461
J	470/470

Bird
U	726/726
V	201/220
b	220/220
c	260/260
e	210/210

Border
—	744/744

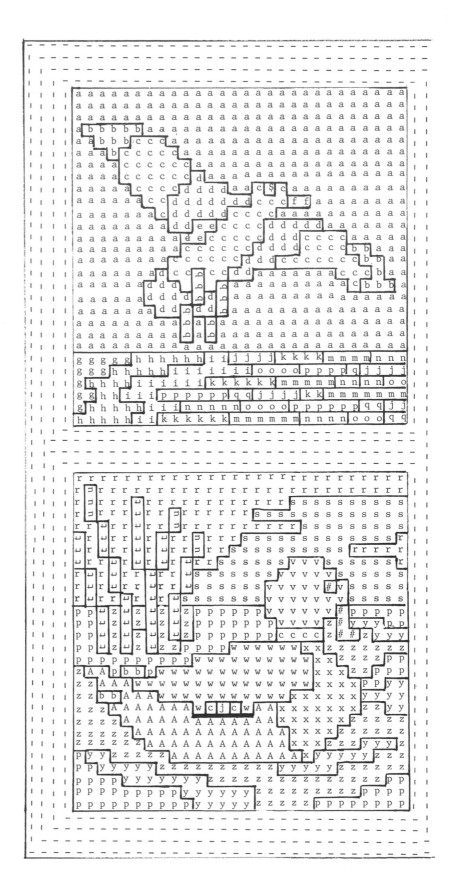

Illus. 28. Chart for Four Birds,
continued on facing page.

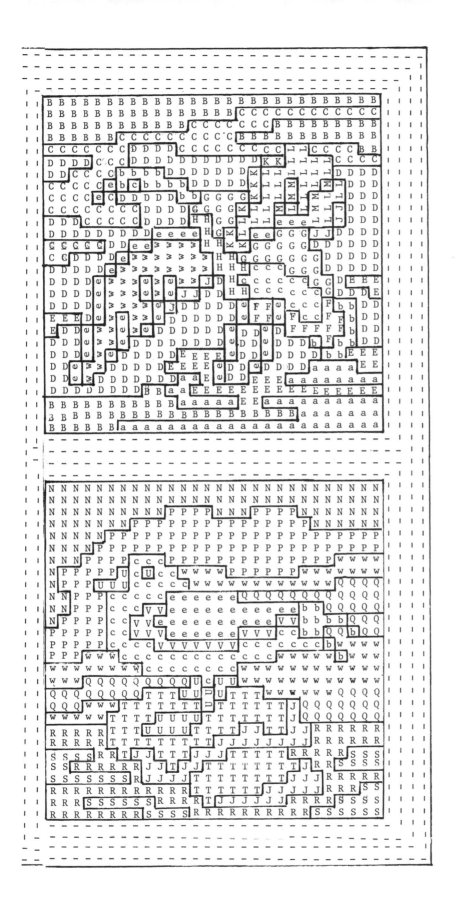

9: Amish Baskets

Shown in color on page C of the color section.

This design is derived from a traditional quilt pattern—one of the ever popular variations of baskets. But the color scheme is a fresh up-to-the-minute one that was suggested by the vibrant color schemes in Amish quilts.

CANVAS
Penelope canvas, 6½ pairs of canvas threads per inch ("6.5-mesh"); cut 13 × 13 inches.

NUMBER OF STITCHES AND ROWS
64 × 64 (size of finished work: approximately 10 × 10 inches).

COLOR SCHEME

–	burgundy	900/900
=	medium purplish red	941/941
X	black	220/220
1	lilac	302/302
2	bluish purple	332/332
3	light purple	304/304
4	reddish purple	353/353
5	medium green	692/692
6	yellowish green	634/634
7	avocado	693/693
8	light green	635/635

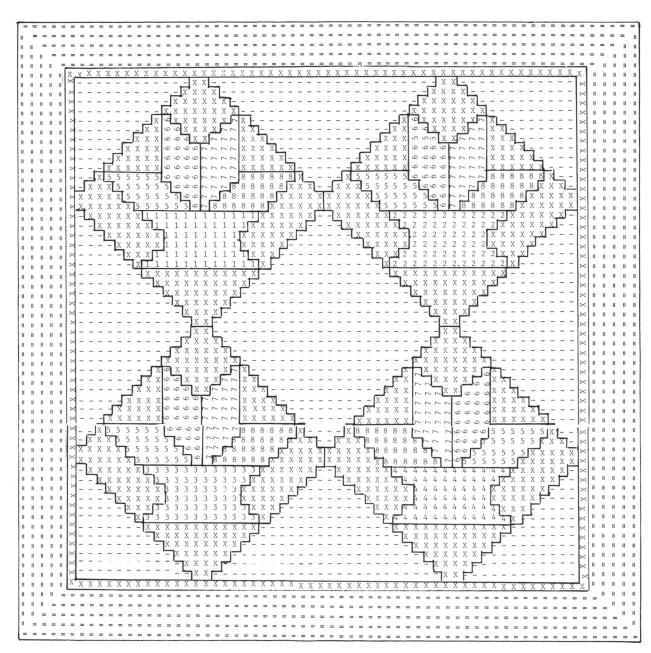

Illus. 29. Chart for Amish Baskets.

10: Grey Skies Over the Golden Gate

Shown in color on page H of the color section.

If all the weathermen keep referring to San Francisco's climate as "Mediterranean" and misty, why do all the photographs always show the Golden Gate Bridge in bright sunlight? My recollection of San Francisco, which admittedly goes back to the early 1940's of World War II, when I was stationed for a while at the Presidio of San Francisco, is that there was a lot of fog in the mornings. Every time that a scene of the Golden Gate Bridge appears on television, one of the kids says, "Yeah, we know, Dad! You used to have to put on all your gear and go hiking up to the crest of the span and then run the rest of the way down to the other end." My recollection is fading, so I don't *think* that we did it every other day, or every other Saturday, but it was often enough! And usually (or is my recollection playing tricks with me?) it was foggy. Therefore, any set of scenes of my favorite American cities in a book to acquaint needleworkers with braided cross-stitch has to include San Francisco as I remember it.

CANVAS

Penelope canvas, 6½ pairs of canvas threads per inch (6.5-mesh); cut 10 × 14 inches.

NUMBER OF STITCHES AND ROWS

48 × 71 (size of finished work: 7 × 10½ inches).

COLOR SCHEME

	Bridge	
B	rust	930/930
b	rust & brown	930/470
	Cables	
C	brown	470/470
c	medium rust & tan	860/872
	Sky	
S	dark grey	202/202
k	dark & medium grey	202/203
K	light grey	203/203
y	2 dark greys	202/210
	Roadway	
r	two light greys	203/256
	Water	
w	two dark blues	580/510
W	dark blue-grey	210/210
	Grass	
g	two dark greens	600/610
	Cars	
X	dark blue	580/580
Z	another dark blue	510/510

Embroidery:

Backstitch (1 strand in needle) tops of far support in rust (930); waterline of boat in red (970).

Illus. 30. On facing page: Chart for Grey Skies Over the Golden Gate.

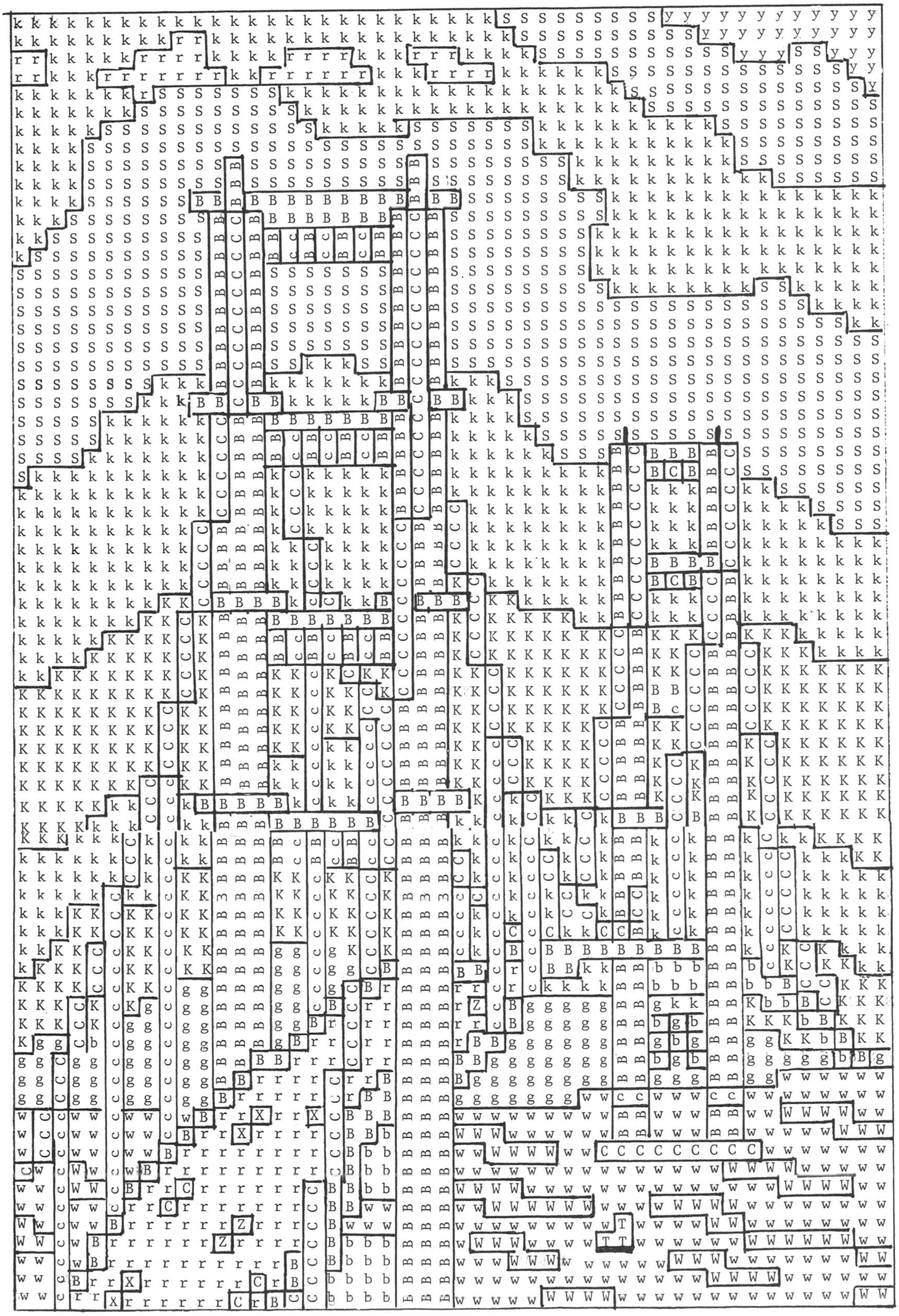

11: Lilies of the Valley

Shown in color on page F of the color section.

I grabbed a few lilies of the valley from the north side of the house, where they grow more luxuriantly than elsewhere. I stuck them into an old cobalt-blue inkbottle that we bought at some flea market years ago, and Mother Nature provided me with another perfect scene. The delicacy of the flowers suggested a small-scale rendition, so I decided to use canvas with more holes per inch.

CANVAS

"Waste canvas" (see *Q&A* 3)—Penelope canvas, 12 pairs of canvas threads per inch (12-mesh); cut 7 × 8 inches.

NUMBER OF STITCHES AND ROWS

51 × 62 (size of finished work: 4 × 5 inches).

COLOR SCHEME

Use a *single* ply of yarn in the needle in the following colors:

Flowers and buds

—	cream	261
b	pale yellow (*b*ud)	715
s	medium green (*s*tem)	693
$	darker green	692

Ink bottle

N	*n*avy blue	571
B	*b*right blue	541
P	*p*urplish blue	342

Wall and table

=	light aqua	585
T	*t*an	436

Embroidery

After braided cross-stitch is completed, make highlights in cream (261)—straight stitches with one ply of yarn in needle.

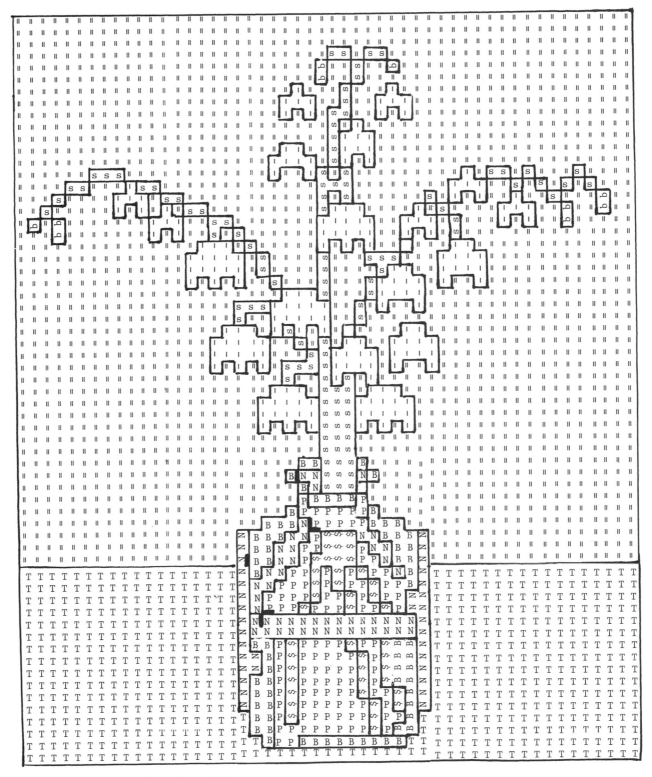

Illus. 31. Chart for Lilies of the Valley.

12: Log Cabin

Shown in color on page A of the color section.

Here is another traditional quilt pattern with infinite design capabilities. It is "traditional" to have the center square in each *Log Cabin* block either red or yellow, representing the fire in the hearth around which the "logs" of the quilt block are added. This block has a diagonal of red squares, or of brown squares, with light colors on one side of the diagonal and dark colors on the other side. This design is one of the tremendous number of variations that can be produced by turning the individual blocks in different attitudes and altering the position of the light and dark areas.

If you decide to use this chart but to use your own leftover yarns, or to buy a whole new supply of yarns to execute it in your own special color scheme, you will find that woolen yarns in this design act the same way that fabrics act in *Log Cabin* quilts: A color that you think is definitely light or definitely dark will sometimes appear completely different when used on the other side of the diagonal. The same color yarn may appear either light *or* dark, depending on the colors that it is used next to.

CANVAS
Penelope canvas, 6½ pairs of canvas thread per inch (6.5-mesh); cut 14 × 14 inches.

NUMBER OF STITCHES AND ROWS
72 × 72 (size of finished work: 11 × 11 inches).

COLOR SCHEME

+	dark red	940/940
X	dark brown	470/470

Diagonal of each *Log Cabin* block is made of red or of brown. Strips on one side of diagonal are assorted medium and dark browns, and on other side of diagonal are assorted tans, creams, and yellows.

A	402/402		M	480/480
B	403/403		N	481/481
C	412/412		O	490/490
D	414/414		P	700/700
E	422/422		Q	702/702
F	424/424		R	704/704
G	435/435		S	710/710
H	436/436		T	712/712
I	445/445		U	743/743
J	461/461		V	753/753
K	472/472		W	754/754
L	475/475		Y	761/761
			Z	771/771
			a	870/870
			b	880/880
			c	881/881

Chart for project on pages 52 and 53.

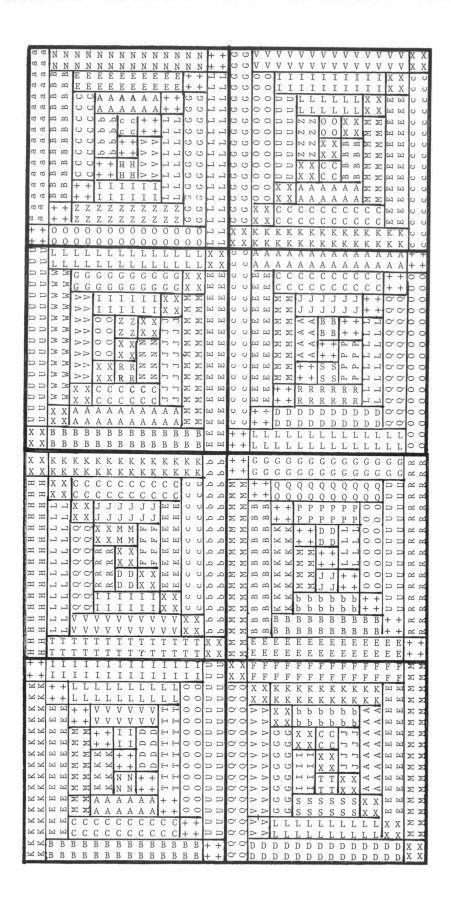

Illus. 32. Chart for Log Cabin,
continued on facing page.

52

13: Maine Lighthouse

Shown in color on page E of the color section.

This design is based on a photograph of a lighthouse "somewhere on the coast of Maine." It looks to me like Nubble Light, outside of York Beach, Maine. But I could be wrong.

CANVAS

Penelope canvas, 6½ pairs of canvas threads per inch (6.5-mesh); cut 12 × 12 inches.

NUMBER OF STITCHES AND ROWS

60 × 59 (size of finished work: 9 × 9 inches).

COLOR SCHEME

A	light blue	546/546
a	grey & light blue	204/546
B	medium blue	545/545
b	medium & light blue	545/546
c	medium blue & aqua	546/584
D	dark brown	470/470
E	black	220/220
F	dark grey	202/202
G	white	260/260
h	medium & dark grey	202/210
J	medium grey	204/204
k	brown & dark red	470/930
L	bright red	841/841
M	dark red	930/930
N	ivory	262/262
P	medium & dark grey	202/204
q	bright & dark red	841/930
r	dark grey & brown	210/470
s	olive & chartreuse	642/693
T	forest green	601/601
U	olive	642/642
v	light & pink tan	436/490
w	dark grey & pink tan	202/490
x	dark grey & med. brown	210/461
y	grey & tan	204/490
Z	bright blue	541/541

Embroidery

Diagram as given produces a flag with three stripes. To make flag more realistic, use a single ply of white (260) to make a backstitch in the center of each red stitch; and a single ply of bright red (841) to make a backstitch in the center of each white stitch.

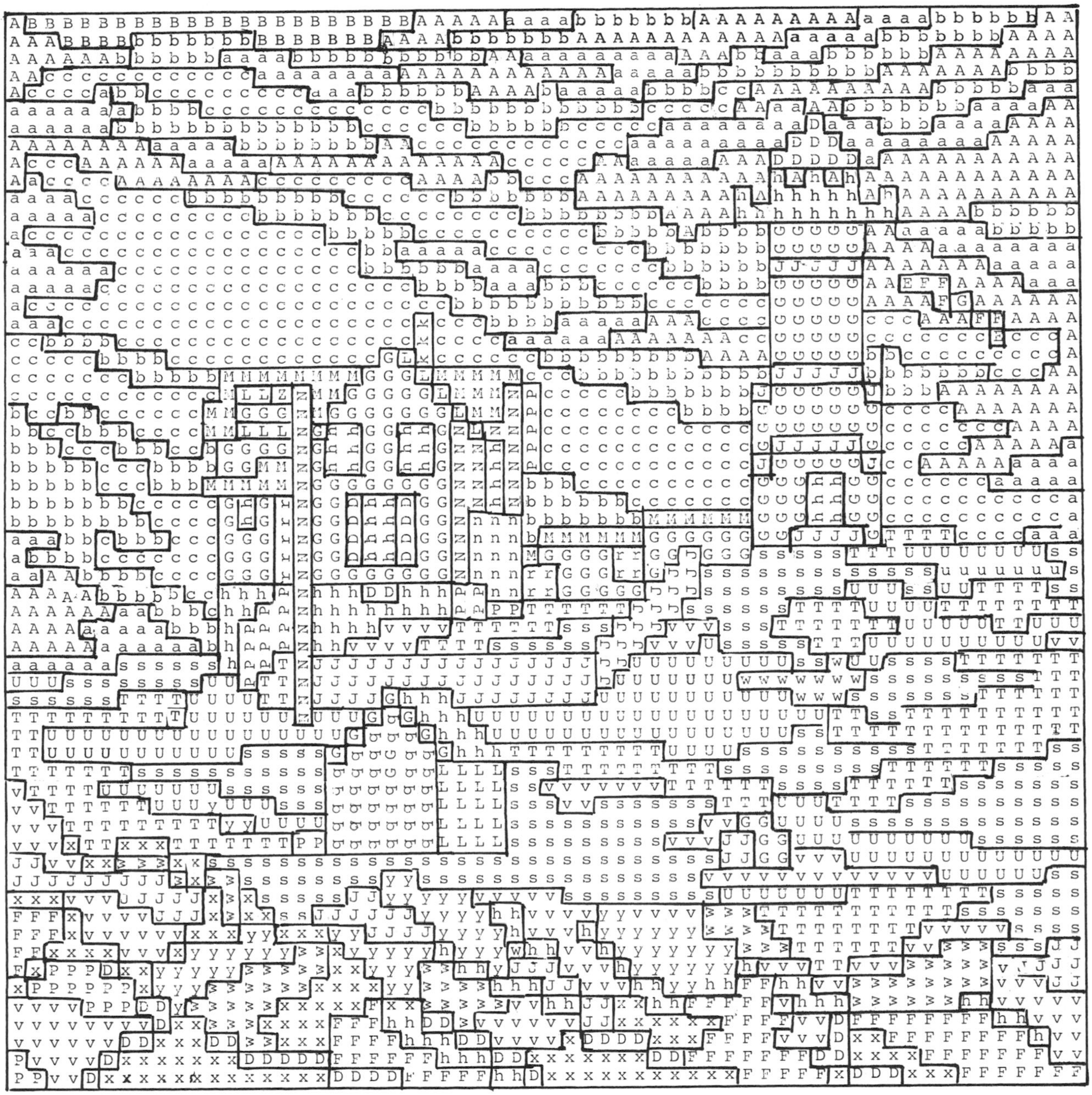

Illus. 33. Chart for **Maine Lighthouse.**

14: Mary's Rabbit

Shown in color on page G of the color section.

All right, I'll admit it right now! It doesn't make sense for you, as a proud parent or grandparent, to reproduce some other kid's scribble-scrabble when you've got dozens, maybe even hundreds, of even cuter drawings done by your own "budding artist." Why, then, did I include this piece? So that it would encourage you to take one of those treasures out of its folder and turn it into a picture. Wouldn't you like to reproduce a kid's drawing and then hear one of her sisters say, as Mary's sister Jean said, "Dad, if Mary doesn't want that, I'd *love to* have it!" Can anything that brings family members closer together really be that bad?

CANVAS

Penelope canvas, 6½ pairs of canvas threads per inch (6.5-mesh); cut 11 × 14 inches.

NUMBER OF STITCHES AND ROWS

52 × 80 (size of finished work: 8 × 12 inches).

COLOR SCHEME

	Sky and clouds	
—	white	260/260
a	grey & lavender	212/342
b	two greys	203/212
c	medium and light blue	544/546
d	copen & aqua	503/593
E	cream	716/716
Y	bright yellow	760/760
	Field	
f	light green	635/635
g	medium green	634/634
h	darker green & cream	694/716
	Rabbit	
—	white	260/260
X	aqua	593/593
	Embroidery	

After piece is worked, backstitch with 1 ply of 593 and 1 ply of 503 in needle, to outline entire rabbit and to define head, tail, etc.

It's always presumptuous for an adult—however proud a parent that person is—to try to reproduce a treasured drawing that had been scribbled with such perfect spontaneity and dramatic sense by a child's hand. But I can't be selfish and simply keep Mary's drawing for myself for ever and ever: Rendering it in braided cross-stitch, enables me to share it with others. Is the rabbit, in that broad field of deep grass, really Mary? Or is it every five-year-old child, including yours? Mary is now a sophisticated 24-year-older, but still as alert and self-assured in her environment as her little "bunny wabbit" was.

Illus. 34. On facing page: Chart for Mary's Rabbit.

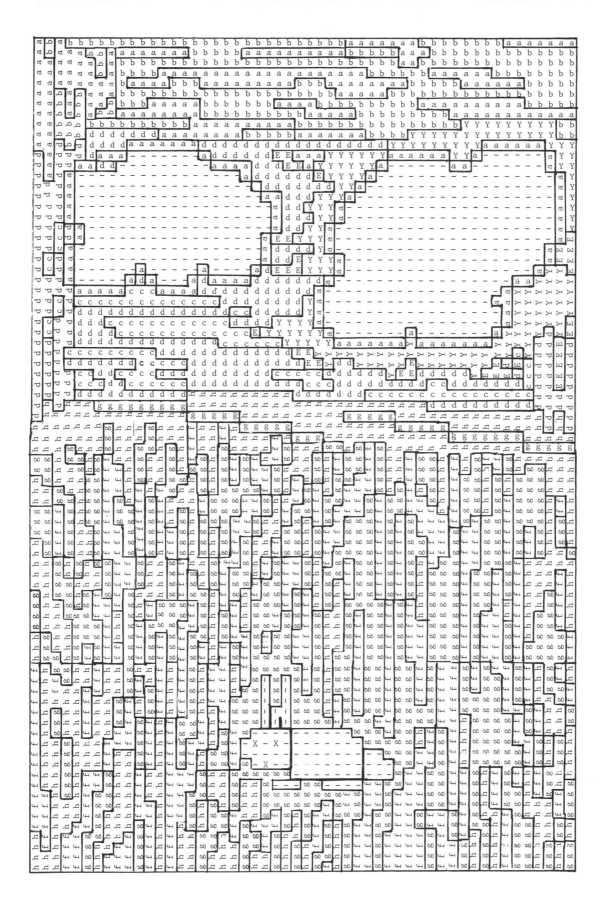

57

15: New Orleans

Shown in color on page H of the color section.

A few years ago I made a patchwork wall hanging called *New Orleans Street Scene*, using a modified version of Seminole patchwork to create the effect of the facade of a building with a wrought-iron balcony. (The wall hanging was printed in color in the June 1982 issue of *Quilter's Newsletter Magazine*.) For this braided cross-stitch version of essentially the same scene, I mentally "took a walk around the corner" and looked at the building from a different angle. Maybe in a few more years I'll take another look at the same scene—either by taking another trip to New Orleans and inspecting the scene, or by mentally repositioning myself—and rendering it in whatever my needlework passion will be at that time. If Monet could keep coming back to those water lilies over and over again, I don't see why I can't keep taking fresh looks at a few favorite scenes of my own.

CANVAS

Penelope canvas, 6½ pairs of canvas threads per inch (6.5-mesh); cut 10 × 12 inches.

NUMBER OF STITCHES AND ROWS

42 × 56 (size of finished work: 6½ × 8½ inches).

COLOR SCHEME

S	*s*ky (blue)	545/545
r	*r*oofline (dark grey)	202/210
F	*f*ascia (mustard yellow)	751/751
t	*t*rim (dark brown)	220/424
b	*b*uilding (orange-brown)	424/642
—	grillework (white)	261/261
P	*p*ainted trim (rust)	721/721
d	*d*oors (greenish-grey)	201/651
w	side*w*alk (light grey)	436/712
c	*c*urb (medium grey)	202/203
=	street (yellow-tan)	436/712

Adjacent building
(three shades of grey):

1	203/203
2	210/210
3	202/202

Embroidery

In right-most window, straight-stitches in *d* between two completed rows of braided cross-stitch *P*.

Illus. 35. On facing page: Chart for New Orleans.

59

16: Ohio Star of India

Shown in color on page E of the color section.

At the 1985 Folklife Festival on the Mall in Washington, D. C., one of the attractions was an open-air market that had been brought from India, together with the artisans and their booths. The entire Indian compound was surrounded by a "fence" made of panels of fabric approximately 4 feet wide and eight feet high. The panels, in pinks, oranges, and purples, had apparently taken a beating in the hot Indian sun, and the colors were of a strange quality—vibrant and muted at the same time, rather like an Indian curry with its mixture of spices that work on the taste buds in different parts of the mouth.

Several of the panels incorporated patchwork motifs, including that universal motif—the eight-pointed star (or *Ohio Star*, as quilters call it). In my version of *Ohio Star of India* the colors are bolder than the muted colors of the fabric "fence"—but maybe the original colors of the fence had been that bold before they were bleached by the sun.

CANVAS
Penelope canvas, 6½ pairs of canvas thread per inch (6.5-mesh); cut 12 × 12 inches.

NUMBER OF STITCHES AND ROWS
59 × 59 (size of finished work: 9 × 9 inches).

COLOR SCHEME

–	dark purple	310/310
R	*red*	970/970
O	*orange*	821/821
Y	bright *yellow*	760/760
G	light *green*	635/635

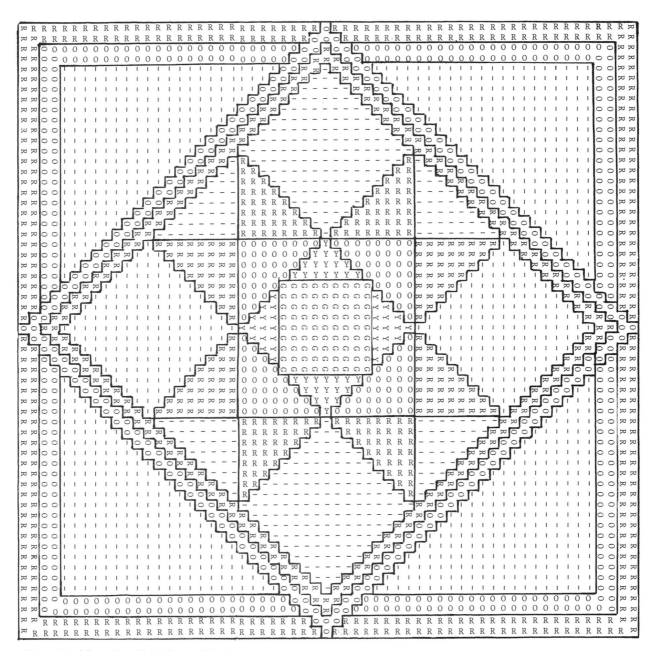

Illus. 36. Chart for Ohio Star of India.

17: Springtime in Patchwork Valley

Shown in color on page G of the color section.

A few years ago Gerry and I attended a quilt seminar in North Carolina, with each of us taking the workshops that we preferred. The workshops I attended included one with Nancy Halpern, who is well known among quilters as a talented artist. As each of us entered the room, we were told to select a slip of paper that looked like the piece of paper you find in a fortune cookie. My slip read *Flowers in the Valley*. Early in her presentation, Nancy told us that the slips of paper represented titles of Irish folk tunes from a book that she had. The title each person picked would be the springboard for the person's imagination in producing an original quilt design.

After Nancy had explained to us her theories of constructing patchwork pictures, we were supposed to doodle around and see what we could come up with ourselves. Somewhere in the course of doodling around, I got the idea of using a basic module—a square block subdivided into triangular shapes—and then flip-flopping that module

into mirror images, offsetting the module vertically and horizontally, and filling in any odd spaces with sections of the module. The total design would be an abstract representation of mountains. My initial idea was to put flowers at the very bottom of the design, thus following to the letter the assignment of *Flowers in the Valley*.

But before I left the workshop, I had decided that spring flowers should be included in most of the modules, up and down the sides of the mountains. It was that design that I would attempt to execute as a patchwork picture after leaving the seminar. In no time I was buying the fabric to do it. I visualized the sun coming over the mountain from one side. Hence, some of the surfaces of the "mountains" would be light-green prints with yellow in them. Surfaces away from the sun would be darker. Surfaces deep in the mountain "valley" would be the darkest of all. I bought yellow-and-green prints, green-and-green prints, green-and-brown prints, and brown-and-brown prints, in a range of colors from the lightest to the darkest, planning to use one piece, and one piece only, of each print to form my mountain landscape.

I still have all those "mountain prints" among our quilting fabrics and I do intend "someday" (I really do, Nancy!) to make my patchwork version of *Flowers in the Valley*. In the meantime, however, I have translated the scene into braided cross-stitch for this book. My first attempt—influenced by my original concept of using fabric prints—included many areas of blended colors. But the result had so "busy" an effect that the modular structure of the design was obscured. The version in this book has areas of solid color only, and, I think, subtly states that structure.

CANVAS
Penelope canvas, 6½ pairs of canvas threads per inch (6.5-mesh); cut 10 × 12 inches.

NUMBER OF STITCHES AND ROWS
48 × 62 (size of finished work: 7 × 9 inches).

COLOR SCHEME

Various greens, light to dark:

Light:

G	613/613
H	604/604
P	634/634

Medium:

B	698/698
C	697/697
D	621/621
F	670/670
L	694/694
N	632/632
Q	633/633
R	693/693
S	653/653
U	690/690

Dark:

A	696/696
E	680/680
J	601/601
K	691/691
M	692/692
T	650/650

Flowers:

V	light yellow	761/761
W	bright yellow	771/771

Sky:

X	light blue	505/505
Y	grey-blue	515/515

Flower stems:

Z	dark brown	470

(backstitches for flower stems—single ply of yarn in needle. 4 backstitches for long stems; 2 backstitches for short stems.)

Chart for project on page 64.

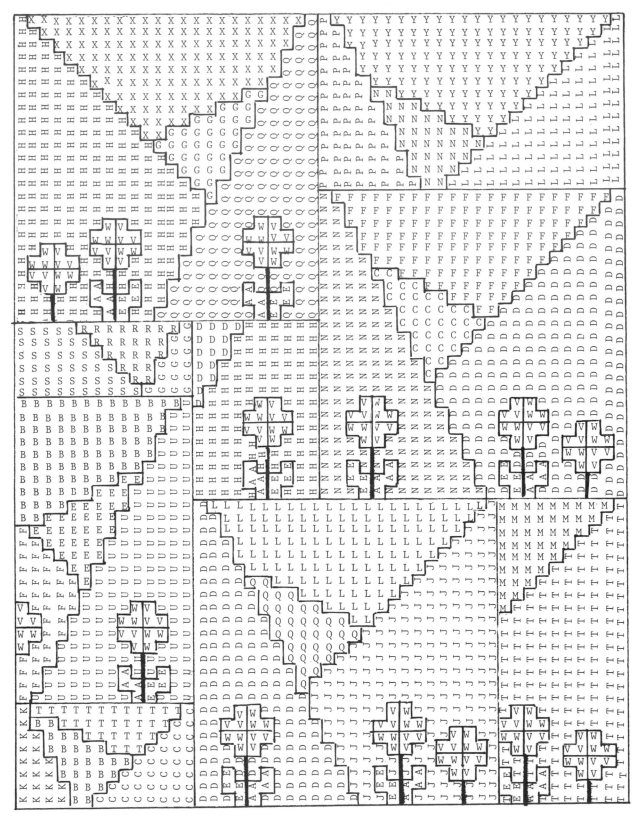

Illus. 37. Chart for Springtime in Patchwork Valley.

64

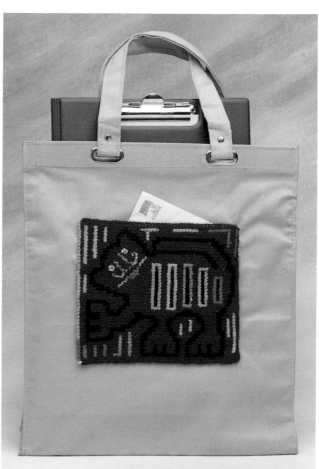

Above: Cat on TV, *a favorite resting place of a favored pet. Instructions start on page 34.*
Above right: Cat Mola—*a different breed of cat and an adaptation of another form of needlework. Instructions start on page 32.*
Right: Log Cabin, *a braided cross-stitch version of the old patchwork classic. See page 50.*

This page shows *different forms of floral art.*
Above: Stained Glass Roses, *which resembles stained glass art. Instructions start on page 80.*
Above right: Spring Flowers, *a landscape. See page 78.*
Right: Roses in a Basket, *a still life. See page 68 for instructions.*

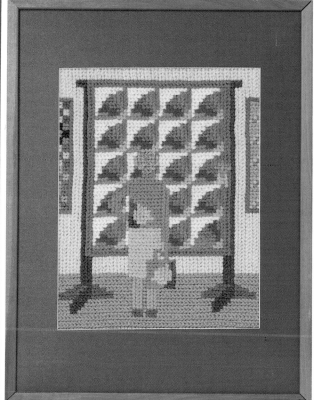

Above left: Amish Baskets. *Instructions start on page 44.*
Above: Star of Bethlehem on Clothesline *was copied from a photograph sent from Germany. Instructions for this design start on page 70.*
Left: Grandmother's Fan Fan. *The title is not a typographical error, but a play on words. See page 25.*

C

Square in a Square in a Square....
Instructions start on page 73.

Trip Around the World. *See page 65.*

Double Irish Chain. *See page 36.*

D

Four Birds. *See page 40.*

Maine Lighthouse. *See page 54.*

Ohio Star of India. *See page 60.*

Seminole Eyeglass Case. *See page 76.*

Washington Mall with Triceratops. *Instructions start on page 82.*

English Sheep. *See page 38.*

Lilies of the Valley. *See page 48.*

F

Bar Harbor. *See page 28.*

Springtime in Patchwork Valley. *See page 62.*

Mary's Rabbit, *a braided cross-stitch rendition of a child's drawing. See page 56.*

G

Grey Skies over the Golden Gate. *See page 46*.

New Orleans. *See page 58*.

Beach House. *See page 30*.

18: Trip Around the World

Shown in color on page D of the color section.

A traditional quilt pattern, executed in colors suggested by the Amish quilt palette.

CANVAS

Penelope canvas, 6½ pairs of canvas threads per inch (6.5-mesh); cut 14 × 14 inches.

NUMBER OF STITCHES AND ROWS

72 × 72 (size of finished work: approximately 11 × 11 inches).

COLOR SCHEME

X	black	220/220
1	light blue	555/555
2	medium blue	502/502
3	dark blue	580/580
4	light peach	845/845
5	medium peach	833/833
6	burnt orange	851/851
7	dark brown	422/422
M	another dark brown	870/870
=	medium grey	210/210

Chart for project on pages 66 and 67.

```
= = = = = = = = = = = = = = = = = = = = = = = = = = = = = = = = = = =
= = = = = = = = = = = = = = = = = = = = = = = = = = = = = = = = = = =
= = = = = = = = = = = = = = = = = = = = = = = = = = = = = = = = = = =
= = = = = = = = = = = = = = = = = = = = = = = = = = = = = = = = = = =
= = = = = = = = = = = = = = = = = = = = = = = = = = = = = = = = = = =
= = = = = = = = = = = = = = = = = = = = = = = = = = = = = = = = = = =
= = = = = = = = = = = = = = = = = = = = = = = = = = = = = = = = = = =

|| || || || || || ||  7 7 7 7  6 6 6 6  5 5 5 5  4 4 4 4  X X X X  3 3 3 3  2 2 2 2
|| || || || || || ||  7 7 7 7  6 6 6 6  5 5 5 5  4 4 4 4  X X X X  3 3 3 3  2 2 2 2
|| || || || || || ||  7 7 7 7  6 6 6 6  5 5 5 5  4 4 4 4  X X X X  3 3 3 3  2 2 2 2
|| || || || || || ||  7 7 7 7  6 6 6 6  5 5 5 5  4 4 4 4  X X X X  3 3 3 3  2 2 2 2
|| || || || || || ||  6 6 6 6  5 5 5 5  4 4 4 4  X X X X  3 3 3 3  2 2 2 2  1 1 1 1
|| || || || || || ||  6 6 6 6  5 5 5 5  4 4 4 4  X X X X  3 3 3 3  2 2 2 2  1 1 1 1
|| || || || || || ||  6 6 6 6  5 5 5 5  4 4 4 4  X X X X  3 3 3 3  2 2 2 2  1 1 1 1
|| || || || || || ||  6 6 6 6  5 5 5 5  4 4 4 4  X X X X  3 3 3 3  2 2 2 2  1 1 1 1
|| || || || || || ||  5 5 5 5  4 4 4 4  X X X X  3 3 3 3  2 2 2 2  1 1 1 1  X X X X
|| || || || || || ||  5 5 5 5  4 4 4 4  X X X X  3 3 3 3  2 2 2 2  1 1 1 1  X X X X
|| || || || || || ||  5 5 5 5  4 4 4 4  X X X X  3 3 3 3  2 2 2 2  1 1 1 1  X X X X
|| || || || || || ||  5 5 5 5  4 4 4 4  X X X X  3 3 3 3  2 2 2 2  1 1 1 1  X X X X
|| || || || || || ||  4 4 4 4  X X X X  3 3 3 3  2 2 2 2  1 1 1 1  X X X X  6 6 6 6
|| || || || || || ||  4 4 4 4  X X X X  3 3 3 3  2 2 2 2  1 1 1 1  X X X X  6 6 6 6
|| || || || || || ||  4 4 4 4  X X X X  3 3 3 3  2 2 2 2  1 1 1 1  X X X X  6 6 6 6
|| || || || || || ||  4 4 4 4  X X X X  3 3 3 3  2 2 2 2  1 1 1 1  X X X X  6 6 6 6
|| || || || || || ||  X X X X  3 3 3 3  2 2 2 2  1 1 1 1  X X X X  6 6 6 6  5 5 5 5
|| || || || || || ||  X X X X  3 3 3 3  2 2 2 2  1 1 1 1  X X X X  6 6 6 6  5 5 5 5
|| || || || || || ||  X X X X  3 3 3 3  2 2 2 2  1 1 1 1  X X X X  6 6 6 6  5 5 5 5
|| || || || || || ||  X X X X  3 3 3 3  2 2 2 2  1 1 1 1  X X X X  6 6 6 6  5 5 5 5
|| || || || || || ||  3 3 3 3  2 2 2 2  1 1 1 1  X X X X  6 6 6 6  5 5 5 5  4 4 4 4
|| || || || || || ||  3 3 3 3  2 2 2 2  1 1 1 1  X X X X  6 6 6 6  5 5 5 5  4 4 4 4
|| || || || || || ||  3 3 3 3  2 2 2 2  1 1 1 1  X X X X  6 6 6 6  5 5 5 5  4 4 4 4
|| || || || || || ||  3 3 3 3  2 2 2 2  1 1 1 1  X X X X  6 6 6 6  5 5 5 5  4 4 4 4
|| || || || || || ||  2 2 2 2  1 1 1 1  X X X X  6 6 6 6  5 5 5 5  4 4 4 4  X X X X
|| || || || || || ||  2 2 2 2  1 1 1 1  X X X X  6 6 6 6  5 5 5 5  4 4 4 4  X X X X
|| || || || || || ||  2 2 2 2  1 1 1 1  X X X X  6 6 6 6  5 5 5 5  4 4 4 4  X X X X
|| || || || || || ||  2 2 2 2  1 1 1 1  X X X X  6 6 6 6  5 5 5 5  4 4 4 4  X X X X
|| || || || || || ||  1 1 1 1  X X X X  6 6 6 6  5 5 5 5  4 4 4 4  X X X X  2 2 2 2
|| || || || || || ||  1 1 1 1  X X X X  6 6 6 6  5 5 5 5  4 4 4 4  X X X X  2 2 2 2
|| || || || || || ||  1 1 1 1  X X X X  6 6 6 6  5 5 5 5  4 4 4 4  X X X X  2 2 2 2
|| || || || || || ||  1 1 1 1  X X X X  6 6 6 6  5 5 5 5  4 4 4 4  X X X X  2 2 2 2
|| || || || || || ||  2 2 2 2  1 1 1 1  X X X X  6 6 6 6  5 5 5 5  4 4 4 4  X X X X
|| || || || || || ||  2 2 2 2  1 1 1 1  X X X X  6 6 6 6  5 5 5 5  4 4 4 4  X X X X
|| || || || || || ||  2 2 2 2  1 1 1 1  X X X X  6 6 6 6  5 5 5 5  4 4 4 4  X X X X
|| || || || || || ||  3 3 3 3  2 2 2 2  1 1 1 1  X X X X  6 6 6 6  5 5 5 5  4 4 4 4
|| || || || || || ||  3 3 3 3  2 2 2 2  1 1 1 1  X X X X  6 6 6 6  5 5 5 5  4 4 4 4
|| || || || || || ||  3 3 3 3  2 2 2 2  1 1 1 1  X X X X  6 6 6 6  5 5 5 5  4 4 4 4
|| || || || || || ||  3 3 3 3  2 2 2 2  1 1 1 1  X X X X  6 6 6 6  5 5 5 5  4 4 4 4
|| || || || || || ||  X X X X  3 3 3 3  2 2 2 2  1 1 1 1  X X X X  6 6 6 6  5 5 5 5
|| || || || || || ||  X X X X  3 3 3 3  2 2 2 2  1 1 1 1  X X X X  6 6 6 6  5 5 5 5
|| || || || || || ||  X X X X  3 3 3 3  2 2 2 2  1 1 1 1  X X X X  6 6 6 6  5 5 5 5
|| || || || || || ||  X X X X  3 3 3 3  2 2 2 2  1 1 1 1  X X X X  6 6 6 6  5 5 5 5
|| || || || || || ||  4 4 4 4  X X X X  3 3 3 3  2 2 2 2  1 1 1 1  X X X X  6 6 6 6
|| || || || || || ||  4 4 4 4  X X X X  3 3 3 3  2 2 2 2  1 1 1 1  X X X X  6 6 6 6
|| || || || || || ||  4 4 4 4  X X X X  3 3 3 3  2 2 2 2  1 1 1 1  X X X X  6 6 6 6
|| || || || || || ||  4 4 4 4  X X X X  3 3 3 3  2 2 2 2  1 1 1 1  X X X X  6 6 6 6
|| || || || || || ||  5 5 5 5  4 4 4 4  X X X X  3 3 3 3  2 2 2 2  1 1 1 1  X X X X
|| || || || || || ||  5 5 5 5  4 4 4 4  X X X X  3 3 3 3  2 2 2 2  1 1 1 1  X X X X
|| || || || || || ||  5 5 5 5  4 4 4 4  X X X X  3 3 3 3  2 2 2 2  1 1 1 1  X X X X
|| || || || || || ||  5 5 5 5  4 4 4 4  X X X X  3 3 3 3  2 2 2 2  1 1 1 1  X X X X
|| || || || || || ||  6 6 6 6  5 5 5 5  4 4 4 4  X X X X  3 3 3 3  2 2 2 2  1 1 1 1
|| || || || || || ||  6 6 6 6  5 5 5 5  4 4 4 4  X X X X  3 3 3 3  2 2 2 2  1 1 1 1
|| || || || || || ||  6 6 6 6  5 5 5 5  4 4 4 4  X X X X  3 3 3 3  2 2 2 2  1 1 1 1
|| || || || || || ||  6 6 6 6  5 5 5 5  4 4 4 4  X X X X  3 3 3 3  2 2 2 2  1 1 1 1
|| || || || || || ||  7 7 7 7  6 6 6 6  5 5 5 5  4 4 4 4  X X X X  3 3 3 3  2 2 2 2
|| || || || || || ||  7 7 7 7  6 6 6 6  5 5 5 5  4 4 4 4  X X X X  3 3 3 3  2 2 2 2
|| || || || || || ||  7 7 7 7  6 6 6 6  5 5 5 5  4 4 4 4  X X X X  3 3 3 3  2 2 2 2
|| || || || || || ||  7 7 7 7  6 6 6 6  5 5 5 5  4 4 4 4  X X X X  3 3 3 3  2 2 2 2

= = = = = = = = = = = = = = = = = = = = = = = = = = = = = = = = = = =
= = = = = = = = = = = = = = = = = = = = = = = = = = = = = = = = = = =
= = = = = = = = = = = = = = = = = = = = = = = = = = = = = = = = = = =
= = = = = = = = = = = = = = = = = = = = = = = = = = = = = = = = = = =
= = = = = = = = = = = = = = = = = = = = = = = = = = = = = = = = = = =
= = = = = = = = = = = = = = = = = = = = = = = = = = = = = = = = = = =
= = = = = = = = = = = = = = = = = = = = = = = = = = = = = = = = = = =
```

Illus. 38. Chart for Trip Around the World, *continued on facing page.*

```
1 1 1 1  2 2 2 2  3 3 3 3  X X X X  4 4 4 4  5 5 5 5  6 6 6 6  7 7 7 7    || || || || || ||
1 1 1 1  2 2 2 2  3 3 3 3  X X X X  4 4 4 4  5 5 5 5  6 6 6 6  7 7 7 7    || || || || || ||
1 1 1 1  2 2 2 2  3 3 3 3  X X X X  4 4 4 4  5 5 5 5  6 6 6 6  7 7 7 7    || || || || || ||
1 1 1 1  2 2 2 2  3 3 3 3  X X X X  4 4 4 4  5 5 5 5  6 6 6 6  7 7 7 7    || || || || || ||
X X X X  1 1 1 1  2 2 2 2  3 3 3 3  X X X X  4 4 4 4  5 5 5 5  6 6 6 6    || || || || || ||
X X X X  1 1 1 1  2 2 2 2  3 3 3 3  X X X X  4 4 4 4  5 5 5 5  6 6 6 6    || || || || || ||
X X X X  1 1 1 1  2 2 2 2  3 3 3 3  X X X X  4 4 4 4  5 5 5 5  6 6 6 6    || || || || || ||
X X X X  1 1 1 1  2 2 2 2  3 3 3 3  X X X X  4 4 4 4  5 5 5 5  6 6 6 6    || || || || || ||
6 6 6 6  X X X X  1 1 1 1  2 2 2 2  3 3 3 3  X X X X  4 4 4 4  5 5 5 5    || || || || || ||
6 6 6 6  X X X X  1 1 1 1  2 2 2 2  3 3 3 3  X X X X  4 4 4 4  5 5 5 5    || || || || || ||
6 6 6 6  X X X X  1 1 1 1  2 2 2 2  3 3 3 3  X X X X  4 4 4 4  5 5 5 5    || || || || || ||
6 6 6 6  X X X X  1 1 1 1  2 2 2 2  3 3 3 3  X X X X  4 4 4 4  5 5 5 5    || || || || || ||
5 5 5 5  6 6 6 6  X X X X  1 1 1 1  2 2 2 2  3 3 3 3  X X X X  4 4 4 4    || || || || || ||
5 5 5 5  6 6 6 6  X X X X  1 1 1 1  2 2 2 2  3 3 3 3  X X X X  4 4 4 4    || || || || || ||
5 5 5 5  6 6 6 6  X X X X  1 1 1 1  2 2 2 2  3 3 3 3  X X X X  4 4 4 4    || || || || || ||
5 5 5 5  6 6 6 6  X X X X  1 1 1 1  2 2 2 2  3 3 3 3  X X X X  4 4 4 4    || || || || || ||
4 4 4 4  5 5 5 5  6 6 6 6  X X X X  1 1 1 1  2 2 2 2  3 3 3 3  X X X X    || || || || || ||
4 4 4 4  5 5 5 5  6 6 6 6  X X X X  1 1 1 1  2 2 2 2  3 3 3 3  X X X X    || || || || || ||
4 4 4 4  5 5 5 5  6 6 6 6  X X X X  1 1 1 1  2 2 2 2  3 3 3 3  X X X X    || || || || || ||
4 4 4 4  5 5 5 5  6 6 6 6  X X X X  1 1 1 1  2 2 2 2  3 3 3 3  X X X X    || || || || || ||
X X X X  4 4 4 4  5 5 5 5  6 6 6 6  X X X X  1 1 1 1  2 2 2 2  3 3 3 3    || || || || || ||
X X X X  4 4 4 4  5 5 5 5  6 6 6 6  X X X X  1 1 1 1  2 2 2 2  3 3 3 3    || || || || || ||
X X X X  4 4 4 4  5 5 5 5  6 6 6 6  X X X X  1 1 1 1  2 2 2 2  3 3 3 3    || || || || || ||
X X X X  4 4 4 4  5 5 5 5  6 6 6 6  X X X X  1 1 1 1  2 2 2 2  3 3 3 3    || || || || || ||
2 2 2 2  X X X X  4 4 4 4  5 5 5 5  6 6 6 6  X X X X  1 1 1 1  2 2 2 2    || || || || || ||
2 2 2 2  X X X X  4 4 4 4  5 5 5 5  6 6 6 6  X X X X  1 1 1 1  2 2 2 2    || || || || || ||
2 2 2 2  X X X X  4 4 4 4  5 5 5 5  6 6 6 6  X X X X  1 1 1 1  2 2 2 2    || || || || || ||
2 2 2 2  X X X X  4 4 4 4  5 5 5 5  6 6 6 6  X X X X  1 1 1 1  2 2 2 2    || || || || || ||
X X X X  2 2 2 2  X X X X  4 4 4 4  5 5 5 5  6 6 6 6  X X X X  1 1 1 1    || || || || || ||
X X X X  2 2 2 2  X X X X  4 4 4 4  5 5 5 5  6 6 6 6  X X X X  1 1 1 1    || || || || || ||
X X X X  2 2 2 2  X X X X  4 4 4 4  5 5 5 5  6 6 6 6  X X X X  1 1 1 1    || || || || || ||
X X X X  2 2 2 2  X X X X  4 4 4 4  5 5 5 5  6 6 6 6  X X X X  1 1 1 1    || || || || || ||
2 2 2 2  X X X X  4 4 4 4  5 5 5 5  6 6 6 6  X X X X  1 1 1 1  2 2 2 2    || || || || || ||
2 2 2 2  X X X X  4 4 4 4  5 5 5 5  6 6 6 6  X X X X  1 1 1 1  2 2 2 2    || || || || || ||
2 2 2 2  X X X X  4 4 4 4  5 5 5 5  6 6 6 6  X X X X  1 1 1 1  2 2 2 2    || || || || || ||
2 2 2 2  X X X X  4 4 4 4  5 5 5 5  6 6 6 6  X X X X  1 1 1 1  2 2 2 2    || || || || || ||
X X X X  4 4 4 4  5 5 5 5  6 6 6 6  X X X X  1 1 1 1  2 2 2 2  3 3 3 3    || || || || || ||
X X X X  4 4 4 4  5 5 5 5  6 6 6 6  X X X X  1 1 1 1  2 2 2 2  3 3 3 3    || || || || || ||
X X X X  4 4 4 4  5 5 5 5  6 6 6 6  X X X X  1 1 1 1  2 2 2 2  3 3 3 3    || || || || || ||
X X X X  4 4 4 4  5 5 5 5  6 6 6 6  X X X X  1 1 1 1  2 2 2 2  3 3 3 3    || || || || || ||
4 4 4 4  5 5 5 5  6 6 6 6  X X X X  1 1 1 1  2 2 2 2  3 3 3 3  X X X X    || || || || || ||
4 4 4 4  5 5 5 5  6 6 6 6  X X X X  1 1 1 1  2 2 2 2  3 3 3 3  X X X X    || || || || || ||
4 4 4 4  5 5 5 5  6 6 6 6  X X X X  1 1 1 1  2 2 2 2  3 3 3 3  X X X X    || || || || || ||
4 4 4 4  5 5 5 5  6 6 6 6  X X X X  1 1 1 1  2 2 2 2  3 3 3 3  X X X X    || || || || || ||
5 5 5 5  6 6 6 6  X X X X  1 1 1 1  2 2 2 2  3 3 3 3  X X X X  4 4 4 4    || || || || || ||
5 5 5 5  6 6 6 6  X X X X  1 1 1 1  2 2 2 2  3 3 3 3  X X X X  4 4 4 4    || || || || || ||
5 5 5 5  6 6 6 6  X X X X  1 1 1 1  2 2 2 2  3 3 3 3  X X X X  4 4 4 4    || || || || || ||
5 5 5 5  6 6 6 6  X X X X  1 1 1 1  2 2 2 2  3 3 3 3  X X X X  4 4 4 4    || || || || || ||
6 6 6 6  X X X X  1 1 1 1  2 2 2 2  3 3 3 3  X X X X  4 4 4 4  5 5 5 5    || || || || || ||
6 6 6 6  X X X X  1 1 1 1  2 2 2 2  3 3 3 3  X X X X  4 4 4 4  5 5 5 5    || || || || || ||
6 6 6 6  X X X X  1 1 1 1  2 2 2 2  3 3 3 3  X X X X  4 4 4 4  5 5 5 5    || || || || || ||
6 6 6 6  X X X X  1 1 1 1  2 2 2 2  3 3 3 3  X X X X  4 4 4 4  5 5 5 5    || || || || || ||
X X X X  1 1 1 1  2 2 2 2  3 3 3 3  X X X X  4 4 4 4  5 5 5 5  6 6 6 6    || || || || || ||
X X X X  1 1 1 1  2 2 2 2  3 3 3 3  X X X X  4 4 4 4  5 5 5 5  6 6 6 6    || || || || || ||
X X X X  1 1 1 1  2 2 2 2  3 3 3 3  X X X X  4 4 4 4  5 5 5 5  6 6 6 6    || || || || || ||
X X X X  1 1 1 1  2 2 2 2  3 3 3 3  X X X X  4 4 4 4  5 5 5 5  6 6 6 6    || || || || || ||
1 1 1 1  2 2 2 2  3 3 3 3  X X X X  4 4 4 4  5 5 5 5  6 6 6 6  M M M M    || || || || || ||
1 1 1 1  2 2 2 2  3 3 3 3  X X X X  4 4 4 4  5 5 5 5  6 6 6 6  M M M M    || || || || || ||
1 1 1 1  2 2 2 2  3 3 3 3  X X X X  4 4 4 4  5 5 5 5  6 6 6 6  M M M M    || || || || || ||
1 1 1 1  2 2 2 2  3 3 3 3  X X X X  4 4 4 4  5 5 5 5  6 6 6 6  M M M M    || || || || || ||
```

19: Roses in a Basket

Shown in color on page B of the color section.

In this piece I "played around with squares"—the weave in the basket, the checkered tablecloth, the squarish roses (vaguely suggested by Anne Orr's cross-stitch floral designs). No, the little area of pink is not a "mistake." It is a fallen rose petal. Will you be as surprised to learn, as I had been surprised when I learned it, that when Flemish artists painted still lifes of tremendous bouquets of flowers, those fallen petals didn't just happen to be there on the table? Rather, they "symbolized the evanescence of life."

CANVAS

Penelope canvas, 6½ pairs of canvas threads per inch ("6.5-mesh"); cut 11 × 11 inches.

NUMBER OF STITCHES AND ROWS

50 × 50 (size of finished work: approximately 7½ × 7½ inches).

COLOR SCHEME

	Roses	
.	medium orange pink	952/952
/	medium pink	943/943
x	medium purplish pink	904/904
o	dark purplish pink	902/902
+	dark red	940/940
	Leaves	
A	dark green	600/600
B	medium grey green	601/601
C	medium forest green	690/690
	Basket	
−	light tan	436/436
=	medium tan	412/412
	Wall and tablecloth	
W	*w*hite	260/260
L	*l*ight blue	505/546
M	*m*edium blue	503/503
D	*d*ark blue	580/580

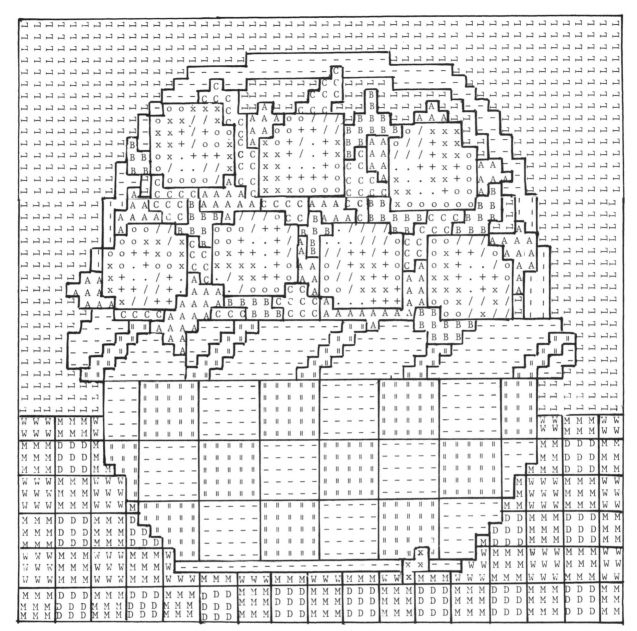

Illus. 39. Chart for Roses in a Basket.

20: Star of Bethlehem on Clothesline

Shown in color on page C of the color section.

A couple of years ago, when I was editor of the quarterly journal of the National Quilting Association—does that explain the preponderance of quilt-related motifs in this book?—I received a letter from an enthusiastic new quilter in Reichelsheim, West Germany, Edel-S. Schneider. Her letter was so informative that I printed it as "Letter from Reichelsheim." Edel had enclosed in her letter several photographs of quilts that she had made. One photograph—*Star of Bethlehem* —appealed to me immediately because it showed her children's legs peeking out from underneath their mother's quilt as they tried valiantly to keep it from flapping in the breeze. They reminded me of *putti*, the pudgy cherubs often depicted in eighteenth-century decorative paintings as they hold up a portrait or a scroll with the name of the noble patron.

I was so charmed by the universality of the scene—I could visualize proud children doing the same thing in Mongolia, Patagonia, and everywhere in between—that I instantly converted the photograph to a braided cross-stitch version that I sent to Edel. In her note back to me, she said, "Sometimes Dirk and Sabine are really angels, but most of the time they are children!" She also said that it had taken three wrong guesses from her husband Peter as to who had done the work, until she asked him, "Why must it be stitched by a woman?" And then she had seen the "Klick." Let's keep those "clicks" (and "Klicks") coming!

CANVAS
Penelope canvas, 6½ pairs of canvas threads per inch (6.5-mesh); cut 12 × 14 inches.

NUMBER OF STITCHES AND ROWS
57 × 73 (size of finished work: approximately 8½ × 11 inches).

COLOR SCHEME

	Quilt	
P	dark *purple*	310/310
L	*lavender*	353/353
O	*orange*-pink	946/946
B	medium *blue*	554/554
R	*rose*-pink	904/904
	Sky and cloud	
s	grey & blue	256/546
K	medium blue	546/546
k	two blues	546/554
Y	bright blue	554/554
w	*white*	260/260

Bushes and grass

1	642/642
2	600/600
3	603/603
4	414/694
5	694/694
6	693/694
7	693/693
8	670/693
9	670/670
m	692/692
r	461/600

Boy and girl

–	light grey	204/204
=	medium grey	201/201
C	orange-brown	881/881
F	medium brown	481/481
Q	dark blue	580/580
H	purplish red	902/902
z	dark brown	461/461
v	brown & red	461/902
n	pink	692/692

Clothesline

T	tan	414/414

Four corner blocks of P in the quilt are made in two directions (instead of solid blocks in a single direction) to suggest quilting design.

Chart for project on page 72.

Illus. 40. Chart for Star of Bethlehem on
Clothesline.

72

21: Square in a Square in a Square...

Shown in color on page D of the color section.

"Now *there's* a familiar design!" our son John said, pointing to this pillow. He was right. About ten or twelve years ago I went through a phase of executing quilt designs in knitting (if, like Madame Defarge, I had knitted the dates in as I went, I wouldn't have had to say "about ten or twelve years ago"). At that time I made several knitted blocks in garter stitch. Because of the different "grain" required for the various shapes in each block, I did not use bobbins to do the entire row at a time. Instead, I would do an entire square or triangle in garter stitch in one color, then pick up stitches appropriately and knit on an adjacent garter-stitch square or triangle. The blocks ended up in needlework limbo, with the exception of *Square in Square*. I knitted that one from the center out until it reached the size of a pillow top and I actually made a pillow from it.

It was very easy to take the garter-stitch version to its next transmogrification by simply replacing each knitted stitch by a braided cross-stitch. And that is what I did, matching the colors to the colors in the knit pillow top. No wonder that John recognized the design immediately.

After completing the braided cross-stitch version, I made it into a pillow (for directions, see *Q&A* 38). Any design in this book could be similarly made into a pillow by the same method, adapting it as required to make the desired pillow size (by adding on additional motifs, a border, etc.).

CANVAS

Penelope canvas, 6½ pairs of canvas threads per inch (6.5-mesh); cut 15 × 15 inches.

NUMBER OF STITCHES AND ROWS

79 × 79 (size of finished work: 12 × 12 inches).

COLOR SCHEME

Y	golden *y*ellow	702/702
M	*m*ustard yellow	750/750
R	bright *r*ed	970/970
K	grey and blac*k*	200/220
L	*l*ight blue	544/544
B	bright *b*lue	541/541
G	*g*rey	210/210

Chart for project on pages 74 and 75.

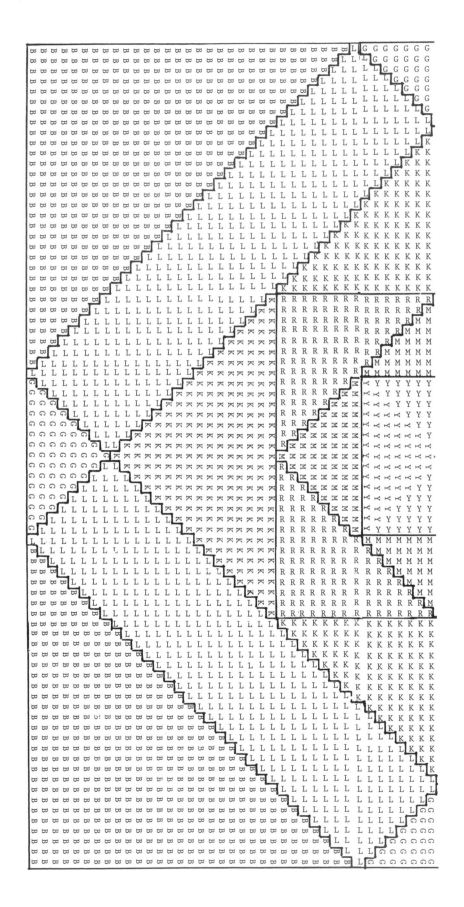

Illus. 41. Chart for Square in a Square in a Square...., *continued on facing page.*

74

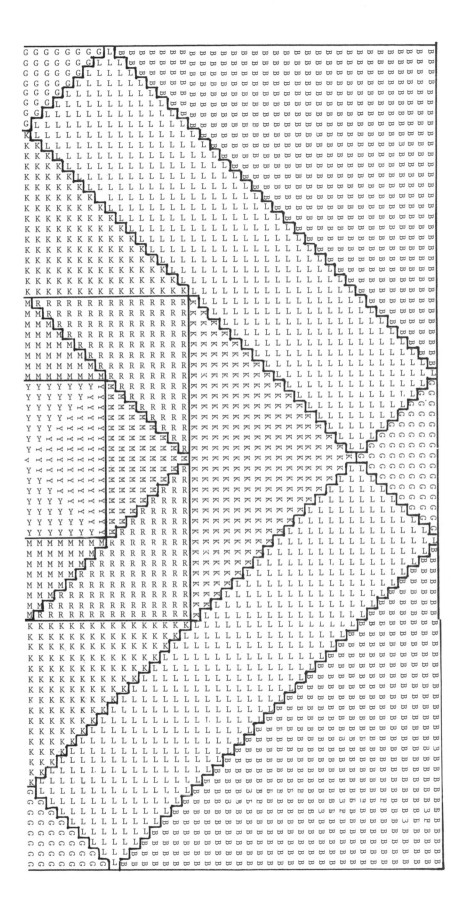

75

22: Seminole Eyeglass Case

Shown in color on page E of the color section.

After this piece was completed, I made it into an eyeglass case (for directions, see *Q&A 38*).

CANVAS

Penelope, 6½ pairs of canvas threads per inch (6.5-mesh); cut 10 × 11 inches.

NUMBER OF STITCHES AND ROWS

54 × 51 (size of finished work: 8 × 7½ inches).

COLOR SCHEME

=	black	220/220
A	bright green	697/697
B	orange-yellow	710/710
C	rust	851/851
D	medium brown	461/461
E	medium blue	583/583
F	bright aqua	591/591
G	orange	811/811
H	chartreuse	693/693
I	forest green	690/690
J	royal blue	541/541
K	pink	963/963
L	lavender	302/302
M	bright red	541/541

For perhaps a century, the Seminole Indians of Florida have made brightly colored bands of patchwork which they appliqué to their clothing. Within the past 25 years or so, there has been much interest among quilters and "patchers" in making this kind of machine patchwork, both in the traditional Seminole designs and in modern, less typically Seminole ones. For this piece I rendered three traditional Seminole designs in bright colors against black, a color scheme that has the same effect in braided cross-stitch that it has in Seminole clothing: the more the bright colors clash with one another, the more harmonious the overall effect against the black. In a well-known photograph of Pablo Picasso, he is wearing what is obviously a Seminole shirt. Need I say more?

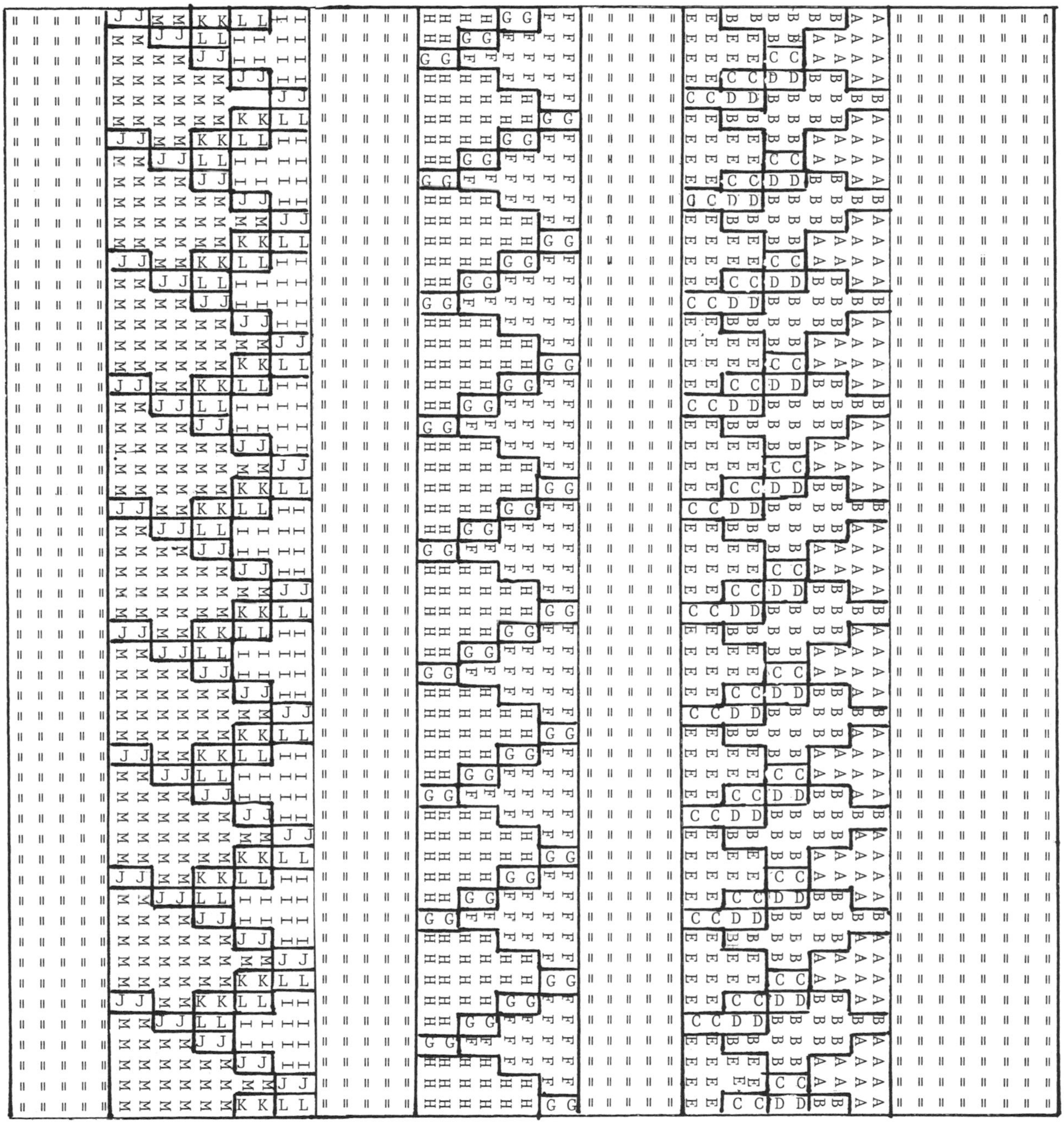

Illus. 42. Chart for Seminole Eyeglass Case.

23: Spring Flowers

Shown in color on page B of the color section.

A lazy gardener's dream—a garden full of bulbs! True, tulips don't grow too well in our heavily compacted clay soil (there doesn't exist enough of anything—of animal, vegetable, or mineral origin—capable of loosening it up). But we do have an abundance of all kinds of narcissus—pale yellow, pale apricot, bright yellow, pure white. And most of them have been in the ground for years and years, leaving me plenty of time year-round to do other things.

Question: Which is easier on the back—doing a bouquet of flowers in braided cross-stitch, or blasting away at the soil to dig out trenches for bulbs, bending over and planting the bulbs, covering them with the tons (it seems like hundreds of tons!) of soil that was removed, fighting the weeds that just *love* to sink their roots into that nicely worked soil? Well, I think you get the idea. Hand me my needle!

CANVAS

Penelope canvas, 6½ pairs of canvas threads per inch (6.5-mesh); cut 9 × 9 inches.

NUMBER OF STITCHES AND ROWS

41 × 41 (size of finished work: 6 × 6 inches).

COLOR SCHEME

	Sky	
a	blues	545/546
	Tulip	
b	dark petals	970/970
c	light petals	972/972
d	stem	750/750
e	leaves	604/663
	Short narcissus	
f	petals	713/713
g	crown	723/723
h	leaves	611/611
	Tall narcissus	
j	petals	715/715
k	middle	613/613
l	leaves	693/693
	Grape hyacinths	
m	dark purple	340/340
n	medium purple	342/342
o	leaves	692/692
	White flowers	
p	petals	260/260
q	center	771/771
r	leaves	662/662
	Small flowers	
n	petals	342/342
i	centers	604/604
	Grass	
s	dark green	690/690
	Earth	
t	two browns	422/461
	Embroidery	

Backstitches to define separate petals. Short narcissus—1 ply of 771. Tall narcissus—1 ply of 723.

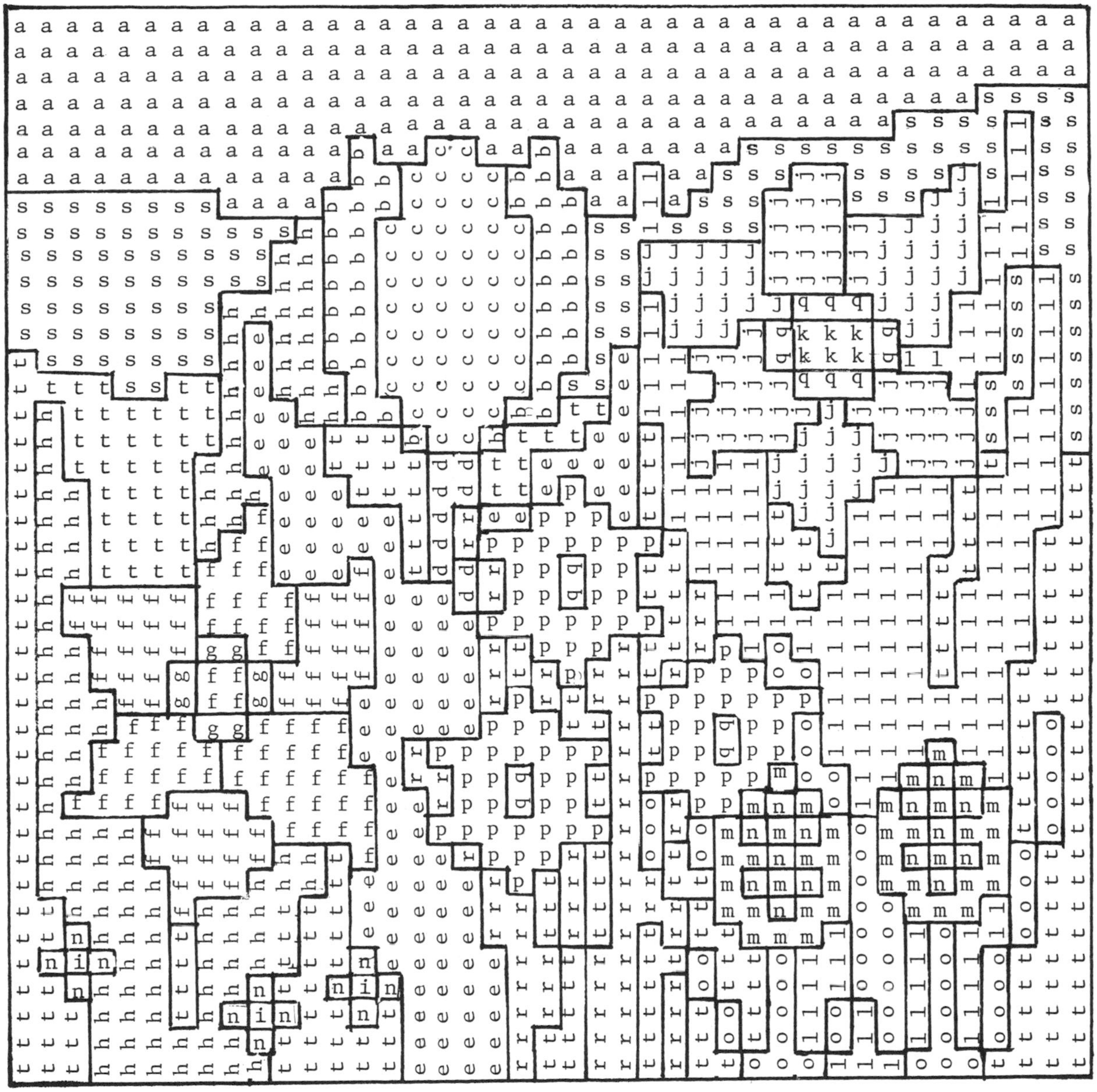

Illus. 43. Chart for Spring Flowers.

24: Stained Glass Roses

Shown in color on page B of the color section.

CANVAS

Penelope canvas, 6½ pairs of canvas threads per inch ("6.5-mesh"); cut 12 × 12 inches.

NUMBER OF STITCHES AND ROWS

61 × 61 (size of finished work: 9 × 9 inches).

COLOR SCHEME

X	black	220/220
Y	*y*ellow	710/710
=	fuchsia	904/904
+	pinkish orange	943/943
–	dusty rose	932/932
R	*r*ed-purple	902/902
B	light *b*lue	505/505
G	dark *g*reen	600/600
M	another dark green	680/680

This design is based on a pieced quilt block that has the appearance of appliqué. In this braided cross-stitch version, the black outlines arouind each element suggest the black strips of bias fabric that are used in the "stained glass" style of quilt-making, which, in turn, imitate the leading in "real" stained glass. Where will all of this end?

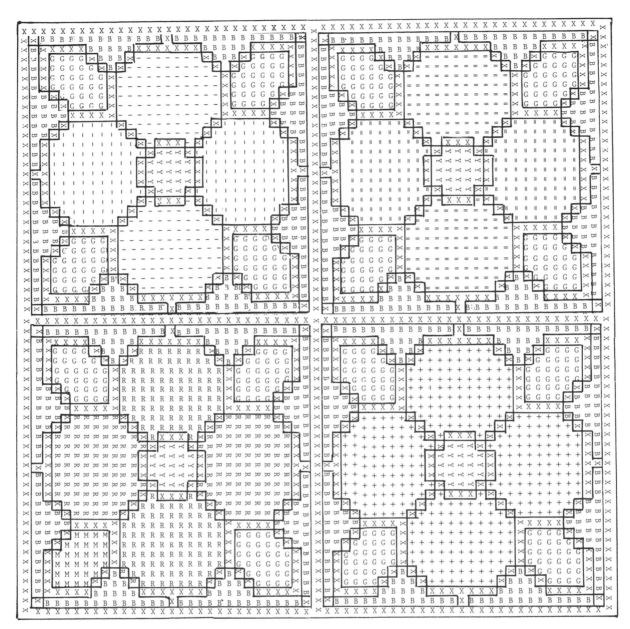

Illus. 44. Chart for Stained Glass Roses.

25: Washington Mall with Triceratops

Shown in color on page F of the color section.

I get tired of looking at all those *Annunciations*, *Assumptions*, *Saint Sebastians*, *Flights into Egypt*, and what-all at the National Gallery, so while my wife tramps gaily through the gallery I usually fritter away the time outside on the Mall, people-watching. On one such occasion I happened to sketch the scene, including the Washington Monument in the distance and the dinosaur in front of the Museum of Natural History in the foreground. After converting the sketch to braided cross-stitch, I thought I'd research that dinosaur, which children love to clamber over while their mothers are looking at all those *Annunciations*, *Assumptions*, *Saint Sebastians*, etc. I learned that it is actually a triceratops and his name is Uncle Beazley, after the hero of *The Enormous Egg*, by Oliver Butterworth. It seems that several years ago a movie (or was it an animated cartoon?) was made from that story, after which the fake triceratops was donated to the Smithsonian Institution, where it has been taking a working-over from the kids ever since.

My wife says that this braided cross-stitch rendition of the scene conveys the sweltering, dusty atmosphere of a summer day on the Mall.

CANVAS
Penelope canvas, 6½ pairs of canvas threads per inch (6.5-mesh), cut 14 × 19 inches.

NUMBER OF STITCHES AND ROWS
103 × 70 (size of finished work: 16 × 10½).

Color scheme

Sky (blue)

a	204/546
b	546/546
c	545/546
d	545/545

Clouds and Washington Monument

g	204/204
w	261/261
y	204/261
–	213/213

Trees (medium and dark greens)

H	690/690
J	600/600
K	601/601
L	692/692
M	670/690
N	601/690
O	690/692
T	441/870
U	441/441

Grass (light greens and yellows)

1	634/703
2	694/694
3	634/634
4	703/745
5	670/670
6	670/694
7	634/694
8	634/670
9	670/703

Museum, cars, etc.

P	204/745
Q	210/213
R	210/210
S	210/721
V	721/721
Y	210/690
Z	751/751
–	213/213
f	875/875
=	210/900
$	721/900

Embroidery

With single ply of R (210) or V (721), make straight stitches as arms and legs of Mall visitors. With single ply of w (261), make straight stitches to form sharper point at top of monument.

Chart for project on pages 84 and 85.

Illus. 45. Chart for Washington Mall with Triceratops, *continued on facing page.*

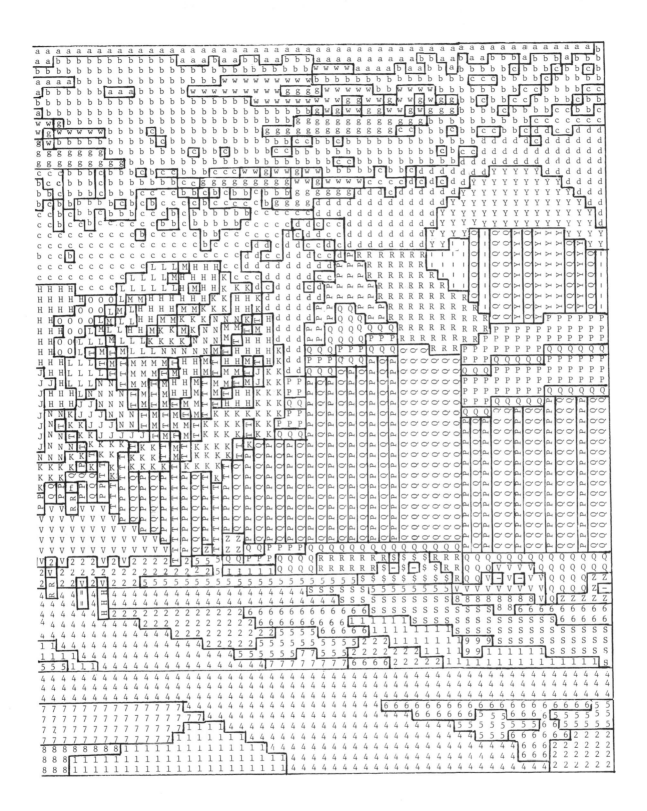

85

· 4 ·
How To Design Your Own Braided Cross-Stitch

Design ideas exist all around you. As you learn to respond to them and execute them, you will begin to feel like a painter who sets up each fresh canvas and asks himself, "What shall I put on it? A still life? A portrait? An abstract design?" Or perhaps an author zipping a fresh piece of paper into his typewriter: "What shall I write? A murder mystery? An article on inflation? A biography of Pushkin?" You have the freedom to choose whatever you want to do. You do not have to go down to the local needlework store and poke around to see what they have for sale. "Here's a counted cross-stitch picture of a Dalmatian! Here's a painted needlepoint canvas for a collie! But," you might tell the owner of the needlework store, "I've got a Weimaraner; you wouldn't happen to have a kit with a picture of a Weimaraner sitting beside a black cat with four white mittens, would you?" Are you kidding? You're going to have to design that yourself!

Now, don't let me hear any of those negative remarks like, "Aw, shucks, Paw, Ah cain't do none of that pitcher-drawin'!" You can, indeed,

with little or no artistic training, transform what you see into braided cross-stitch. It takes just a couple of steps.

Step 1 is *seeing*. It is noticing the artistic possibilities of the life that is teeming all around you. It is isolating from that mass of visual, artistic, and emotional stimuli the particular image you want to record today for your own pleasure or for someone else's. That image can be anything! Maybe it's the pear tree that your son planted. The trunk was hardly bigger than a broomstick then, but now the tree is huge, with beautiful red and gold foliage on the side facing the November sun. It's the prettiest tree on the street! Of course, you can render it in a braided cross-stitch.

I'll admit that it takes a tiny bit of training to see and appreciate beauty everywhere. Many years ago, when I was up to my elbows in rya yarns, one of the children came into the house and said, "Dad, there's a beautiful design for a rug out on the driveway!" And there *was*—a swirl of black against the grey driveway, with iri-

86

descent colors dancing all over the black! How much nicer it was to have someone appreciate and report something as a beautiful design, instead of saying, "Dad, the engine oil has all drained out onto the driveway; they must have forgotten to replace the plug!" Many, many forgettable oil changes later I still remember everyone going out to the driveway and agreeing that that mess was indeed a beautiful design!

But seeing is not enough for the braided cross-stitch designer. A photographer may see a rainbow in drained engine oil and just photograph it! An artist may decide to render the rainbow as an abstract painting. A "painter with yarns" may apply the yarns freely all over the fabric just as the artist applies paints to his canvas. But the braided cross-stitch designer cannot just snap the picture or start splashing colors of yarns around. First the designer has to take Step 2: Breaking the picture down into a grid that produces tiny squares, each specific color in its own specific location, and then transposing each grid square into an individual stitch onto canvas. But craftsmen have been doing that for hundreds or thousands of years! Cross-stitch embroideries, Oriental rug designs, African cowry-bead designs, Finnish weaving designs, Italian Renaissance wood-inlay designs, and ancient Greek and Roman mosaic floors all required the craftsman first to break down an image into multiple fragments and then to reconstitute those fragments (as individual stitches, knots, beads, pieces of yarn, wood, stone, etc.) into a whole. And that process is still going on, not only in the arts and crafts, but also in technology.

I'll bet that you're getting anxious to learn how to design your own braided cross-stitch piece, but I'd like to ask a question: Which came first—art or technology? In this Age of Technology I like to recall that the wonderful world of computers has among its origins a method of using punched cards for processing census data in the late nineteenth century. But that punch-card data-processing method was devised by Hollerith after he was inspired by the punched cards used in Jacquard weaving to produce complicated woven coverlets by machinery. So, in effect, the images we receive from outer space today owe a lot to those technical geniuses, millennia ago, who got the idea of weaving vegetable or animal fibres together in order to get fabrics with which to cover themselves against the cold. Or were they artistic geniuses?

Now that the theorizing and philosophizing are out of the way, let's get down to the mechanics of converting any design to braided cross-stitch. Each of the designs in this book was made in one of the following three ways, each of which will be explained in detail below:

- by plotting a geometric design directly onto graph paper;
- by tracing an already existing photograph or drawing, and transferring that tracing, full size, onto graph paper with the appropriate grid; or
- by making a rough sketch of a real or imaginary scene, and transferring that sketch, full size, onto graph paper with the appropriate grid.

None of these methods are particularly difficult, but there is a still easier method that was not used for this book, and which does not require the use of graph paper. The method, which beginning needleworkers think is the best one for them, is simply to copy someone else's design that has been plotted onto a graph for some other type of needlework (cross-stitch embroidery, Fair Isle knitting, filet crochet, etc.) and to render the graphed symbols in braided cross-stitch. I'll admit that this gets your needle going earlier than the three methods I shall describe, but it does not give you the opportunity to express your own personality, to make your own statements about the specific things that you like. So I hope that you will not dismiss these methods by saying, "Oh, they're just too complicated for me!"

Method 1: Plotting Directly Onto Graph Paper

To plot a geometric design onto graph paper, all you have to do is to decide how large you want the finished version to be, and then draw on the graph paper the squares, triangles, etc. with a number of graph-paper squares that represent the stitches required to fit the canvas size. That sounds a bit complicated, so let's use a simple example. Let's say that you have decided on a design—a "Nine-Patch" (a quilt design, consisting of a large square made up of three rows of three smaller squares), with the center square divided into triangles (Illus. 46).

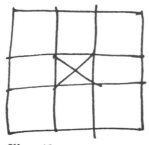

Illus. 46.

If you want your finished piece to be a pillow top 12 inches square, each of the small squares in the Nine-Patch will be 4 inches square; if you want your finished piece to be a 6-inch square that you will make up as a checkbook cover, each small square will be 2 inches square. A 12-inch square of 6.5-mesh Penelope canvas is 78 x 78 stitches (12 x 6.5); a 6-inch square is 39 x 39 stitches (6 x 6.5). Let's say that you decide to "start small"; you're going to make the checkbook cover. On a piece of graph paper with *any* number of squares per inch, draw a large square of 39 x 39 grid squares. Divide that square into thirds; divide the center square into triangles. There's your chart! It shows you that each of the small squares is going to have 13 rows of 13 stitches; two triangles (A) are going to have rows of 13−11−9−7−5−3−1 stitches, and two triangles (B) are going to have 11−9−7−5−3−1 stitches (Illus. 47). Your only problem now is deciding what color yarns to use. Just think of how many quilt designs can be graphed for braided cross-stitch by this easy method!

Some geometric designs are so simple that it is not even necessary to plot them on graph paper: All that is required is to make a *mental* decision about how large to make each square, triangle, etc. For example, for *Trip Around the World*, I sketched onto the back of an envelope the layout I wanted to try: Blocks 1−2−3 in a light-to-dark sequence of blues; blocks 4−5−6−7 in a light-to-

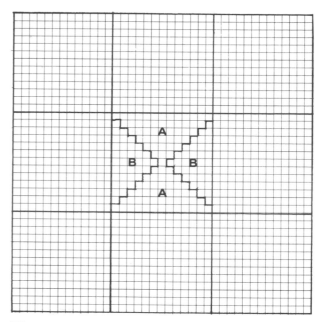

Illus. 47.

dark sequence of oranges; color sequences separated by black diagonals (Illus. 48). All I had to do was to count the number of blocks left-to-right and top-to-bottom: 15 blocks in each direction.

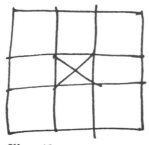

Illus. 48.

My only decision was how many stitches to make each block. Blocks three rows of three stitches would make a finished size too small for my pur-

88

pose, on 6.5-mesh canvas, 15 x 3 = 45 stitches, or 6.92″. I decided to make each block *four* stitches wide: 15 x 4 = 60 stitches, or 9.23″; with a border of 6 stitches all around, the total number of stitches would be 72 x 72, or 11″ square. I did not even have to plot this design onto graph paper, although I did represent each stitch when I drew the chart for this book.

To use another example from this book, *Ohio Star of India* reveals, even in a hurriedly made sketch drawn on a paper napkin at the Folklife Festival, that it is another "square in a square" design consisting of smaller squares and triangles (Illus. 49). The design is somewhat unusual in having two borders around each of the two largest squares. To plot this design I started with the finished size I desired: a 9-inch square. On 6.5-mesh canvas, 9″ = 58.5, or 59 stitches. Allowing one stitch for the center, each side of the finished design would be 29 stitches (29 + 1 + 29 = 59). To plot this design, I drew the first

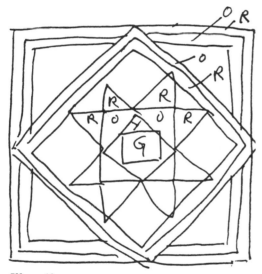

Illus. 49.

main diagonal from the center square; allow a 2-stitch border of red and a 2-stitch border of orange along that diagonal and around the outer edges (Illus. 50); and the remaining squares and

triangles in the design fell into place easily, providing the chart for executing the design.

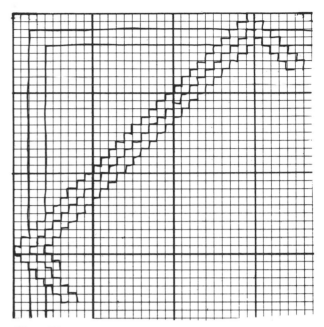

Illus. 50.

The other designs in this book that were done by this method are: *Amish Baskets, Double Irish Chain, Log Cabin, Seminole Eyeglass Case, Springtime in Patchwork Valley., Square in a Square in a Square...*, and *Stained Glass Roses.*

Any geometric design made up of squares, triangles, rectangles, stripes, etc., can be plotted in this way onto graph paper. Incidentally, the number of squares *per inch* on the graph paper that you use has nothing to do with the finished size of your braided cross-stitch piece. Whether you plot, say, 20 stitches on 4-to-the-inch graph paper or 10-to-the-inch graph paper, those 20 squares will represent the same 20 stitches: on 6.5-mesh canvas, those stitches will cover 3 inches. but this "graph-paper grid vs. canvas mesh" distinction will be discussed in more detail in the next section of this chapter.

Method 2: Tracing a Photograph or Drawing

In order to use this method, you must have sheets of fairly rigid transparent plastic. I use plastic "page protectors" (also called "document protectors")—plastic covers, punched with three holes, for protecting looseleaf notebook pages. The protectors can be purchased in any office supplies or school supplies store. Trimming away the side with the punched holes and cutting apart the front and back of the protector yields two pieces of plastic 8½ x 11 inches.

You must also have sheets of graph paper with grids in various sizes. I have a supply of graph paper with 4, 5, 6, 7, 8, 10, 12, and 16 squares to the inch, but I find that the sizes I use most frequently to develop braided cross-stitch designs are 6-to-the-inch, 8-to-the-inch, 10-to-the-inch, and, occasionally, 12-to-the-inch. But you should have the other sizes also available for trial-and-error purposes. The graph paper can be transparent or opaque. Transparent graph paper is easier to use, but is not always available in sizes that you need.

Graph paper with certain numbers of squares per inch is often not available except in artist supply or drafting supply shops. Graph paper purchased there may be considerably more expensive than ordinary graph paper, because of its greater precision—a precision that is not actually needed for our purposes. One way to obtain a good supply of such sizes of graph paper inexpensively is to buy one or two sheets of the "draftsman-quality" graph paper and make multiple copies on a copying machine. Make sure first, however, that the sheets read "reproducible." If you try to make Xerox copies of "non-reproducible" grids, you'll end up with blank paper!

Needlework shops sell kits of transparent plastic sheets onto which grids of various sizes have been printed. One kit contains sheets with 5, 11, 14, 18, 22, and 25 squares per inch; another kit contains sheets with 5, 7, and 10 squares per inch; a third kit contains sheets with 4, 6, 12, 13, 16, 24, 26, 29, 30, and 40 squares per inch. These kits are designed primarily, although not exclusively, for converting photographs or drawings to counted cross-stitch, needlepoint, and petitpoint; hence the preponderance of grid sizes with a rela-

tively large number of squares per inch. Although these kits are fun to work with for other purposes, they are actually not very useful for the method described in this book. Moreover, they lack a grid that I frequently need for this method: 8-to-the-inch.

The procedure involves the following steps, each of which will be described in detail:

- roughly trace onto a sheet of plastic the rough outlines of the picture you want to render in braided cross-stitch;
- overlay onto the tracing, in sequence, sheets of graph paper with various grid sizes until you find the grid that accommodates the picture best;
- determine whether the picture on the selected graph paper covers a number of grid squares (= stitches) that will produce the desired finished size of your piece;
- convert the outlines to the grid format, assigning to the various areas the colors of yarn that you plan to use; and
- use the chart thus produced as your guide for making braided cross-stitches on canvas.

EXAMPLE

Your grandchild (budding artist) draws a picture of your house (A) and sends it to you. You want to reproduce it in braided cross-stitch. Who wouldn't?

Step 1: Put a piece of plastic over the picture and, using a pen with *permanent* black ink (water-soluble ink tends to smudge), roughly trace the picture (B). Put work of art aside for the time being.

Step 2: Overlay a piece of 6-to-the-inch graph paper over the plastic tracing (C) and "see what happens." If the graph paper is transparent, this step is very easy to carry out. If the graph paper is opaque, hold the tracing, together with the piece of graph paper (the "overlay"), over a light table, or over a pane of glass or sheet of Plexiglas with a light shining through it, or against a window—or anything to make the ink outline "shine through" to the grid on the graph paper. Your first reaction: It looks good! The front steps fit in

A
Original work of art

B
Tracing onto transparent plastic

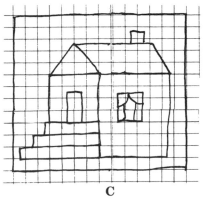

C
Overlay with 6-to-the-inch graph paper

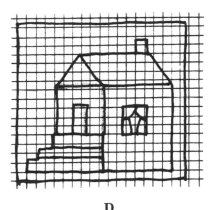

D
Overlay with 8-to-the-inch graph paper

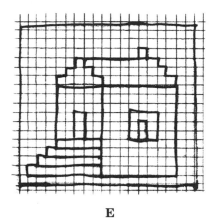

E
First attempt to "square off" design (8-to-the-inch overlay)

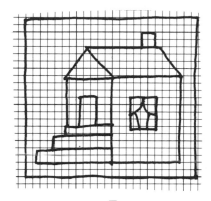

F
Overlay with 10-to-the-inch graph paper

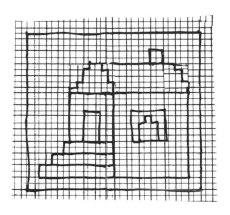

G
Overlay with 12-to-the-inch graph paper, design "squared off"

perfectly! But the roof and the eave are only 2½ grid squares high. Also, front of house is 4 squares wide—door cannot be centered unless you make it two squares wide. Try with a piece of 8-to-the-inch graph paper (D). The roof and eave improve: The eave could be made like ordinary cross-stitch:

```
    X
   XXX
  XXXXX
```

The front of house is now five squares wide; the door could be one stitch wide and centered. But three steps are now out of whack. Could you live with four steps, instead of three? Try graphing it on 8-to-the-inch paper (E) since you like the eave and the front door, but you don't like the steps and the window. Try 10-to-the-inch graph paper (F): The steps are bad. Try 12-to-the-inch: Each step can be two rows high; the door can be three stitches wide, with the wall two stitches wide on each side; the roof can be done in five rows; and the window can be centered in the large wall; the curtains have a better shape (you can add embroidery stitches to define them).

You stop at 12-to-the-inch and ask yourself how large a braided cross-stitch piece this chart will produce. Measure the height and width of the chart (those dimensions, like the traced outlines, have not changed throughout this entire process): height 2¼", width 2⅜". Check the table "From Design to Graph Paper to 6.5-mesh Penelope Canvas" (*Q&A 40*). In the left-hand column, find 2. In column "12-to-the-inch graph paper" you read: 24 squares = 3.7". You have 26 x 28 squares on the graph: size of finished piece, approximately 4" square. You decide to do it (you'll figure out later what you will do about the inscription and the smoke).

Do the final "squaring-off" of the outlines (Illus. 51, G). Roof line and eave have to be "fudged": roof line goes up in increments of 2−2−1; you cannot make a sharp point at the top of eave. Note that, whatever size grid on the graph paper you are using, some elements in the design will fit in well and others will not. You will have to decide which elements in the design are ones that you want to preserve, and which can be adjusted or even distorted. If you have decided to keep the steps as the predominant fea-

ture (and I think they are), then you should choose a grid that accommodates them well. Notice in this example that the number of steps (or of anything else in the original picture) does not necessarily match up with the number of anything else: either the number of squares on the graph paper, or the number of stitches on canvas. In this example, the steps are best rendered on 6-to-the-inch or 12-to-the-inch graph paper.

But what if the picture you wanted to reproduce in braided cross-stitch included an American flag, with its 13 stripes? If you decided that it was essential to render those 13 stripes, and not a stripe less or more, then, whatever the size of the flag in the picture, you would have to use graph paper with a very large number of squares per inch. Assuming that the flag is *exactly* one inch high in the picture (most unlikely!), you would have to overlay a piece of graph paper 13 squares to the inch (or 26-to-the-inch, or any other multiple of 13). If the flag were *exactly* ½" high (again, most unlikely!), the only size grid capable of accommodating 13 stripes in ½" is 26-to-the-inch. If the flag were some odd size (now this *is* likely!), it might be difficult, if not impossible, for you to render the flag in 13 stripes in a braided cross-stitch piece that you are planning. Wouldn't you rather make a flag with seven, five, or three stripes and assume that people would know what it was?

GRAPH-PAPER GRID VS. CANVAS MESH

For some reason, people sometimes become confused about the number of squares on graph paper and the number of stitches on canvas. They think, for example, that if a design has been charted on 8-to-the-inch graph paper, it will produce 8 stitches to the inch on canvas. But it should be apparent that the *representation* of a design in any kind of grid does not have anything to do with the size of that design as executed in any medium. Let's say that you were able to render the American flag in a series of 13 stripes:

```
XXXXXXXXXXXXXXXXXX
··················
XXXXXXXXXXXXXXXXX
```

How would you like that flag as a brooch, with 13 alternating rows of diamonds and rubies? I wouldn't like it; it wouldn't be exactly accurate. You wouldn't be able to count the 50 individual stars.

Or would you prefer to have all the people in your hometown pose for a Fourth of July photograph? Each "X" person could wear a red suit or dress; each "." person could wear a white suit or dress; the 50 "star people" could each wear a navy-blue suit or dress and a white derby. We'd have to take the photograph from a helicopter, but we could do it!

No, I think it would be better to do the same 13 stripes in petitpoint, on 40-to-the-inch canvas! Or in dried kidney beans and dried navy beans, glued to a big piece of plywood....

As you can see, a design that can be conceptualized in the form of a grid can be executed in whatever size you want to, depending on the amount of detail you want to retain, and the size of the basic module in the medium you choose. Many years ago the author H. Allen Smith wrote that his favorite fantasy was to assign the seats in the orchestra for the opening night of the Metropolitan Opera. He would arrange bald-headed men in such a way that, viewed from the balcony, their heads would spell out a certain word, and "the dot on the *i*" would be the then president of Columbia University. Smith must have been a closet cross-stitcher! He certainly understood how to construct a grid!

Back to the Subject, Please!

But to return to the subject: The second method of rendering designs onto graph paper for converting them to braided cross-stitch: After selecting the appropriate grid and converting the tracing to its "squared-off" version, assign the color codings to each area of the design. In the example of your grandchild's drawings of *Gramp's House*, it may be sufficient to label each area to be filled in with a solid color. But if the drawing or photograph has a complicated color scheme, you will have to refer to the original in order to subdivide areas into smaller areas of different hues and shades. The commercial plastic sheets with preprinted grids can be used at this time for the purpose of isolating individual areas of color in the original drawing or photograph, assuming that you can buy a grid corresponding to the grid size of the graph paper that you finally decided to use.

This method was used to make several designs in this book. *English Sheep, Maine Lighthouse,* and *Star of Bethlehem on Clothesline* were traced from photographs; *Mary's Rabbit* was traced from a drawing that my daughter made when she was a child; *Fulmar Petrel* was traced from one of four framed color plates taken from an Audubon book; and *Cat Mola* was traced from a small mola that a member of our quilting group bought in Panama and that she showed me briefly before giving it to her ailurophile grandson. The actual process of converting these photographs and drawings was exactly the same as the one described above. I simply traced roughly the main elements of the picture, and used overlays of various grids of graph paper until I found the grid that best accommodated the details in the scene. Then I subdivided the areas into the individual areas of color-blendings, striving for subtle gradations in sky, grass, water, etc.

The main noteworthy features about *Maine Lighthouse* and *Fulmar Petrel* (Illus. 52) are that the tracing of the Maine landscape was cropped to render the composition as a square; and the tracing of the bird is actually a mirror image of the print. Since the tracings are made on transparent plastic, it is very easy to reverse them, superimpose tracings onto one another, or perform other composition tricks before plotting the picture onto the graph paper. Note that, even though the tracing of the bird is almost the same height as the tracing of the Maine landscape, the finished size of each piece is, respectively, 4½ x 4½ inches, and 9 x 9 inches: the reason is that the bird was plotted onto 6-to-the-inch graph paper, and the Maine landscape onto 8-to-the-inch.

Illus. 51.

Method 3: From Preliminary Sketch to Graph Paper to Braided Cross-Stitch

The method of converting a rough sketch to a graph-paper grid which is, in turn, converted to braided cross-stitch is slightly more complicated than Method 2, which involves tracing a design from a photograph, postcard, drawing made by someone else, or any other traceable picture already in existence. Method 3 requires someone (why not you?) to draw the rough outlines of the scene that you want to reproduce in braided cross-stitch. Either by reproducing the scene right there in front of your eyes, or the scene in your imagination.

There is not enough space in this book to teach you how to sketch, but I can tell you that, for purposes of needlework design, no great skill is required. Any irregularities in your sketch will be adjusted when you transfer the sketch to graph paper. Then, as you transfer the squares in your graph-paper chart to your canvas in the form of braided cross-stitches, you can act confi-dently in a role with which you are familiar— the role of "yarn artist." If, for example, two of the trees are merging together into an indistinct mass on your canvas, change the shape of one of them as you make your stitches—adding more dark foliage here, eliminating some foliage stitches there—until you get the desired effect.

Although the preliminary sketch can be very rough, and, in fact, very small, the most important thing is to make sure that the relationships among the elements in the sketch are preserved: Sizes of objects in relation to other objects, and the perspective of the scene. The best way to preserve these relationships is to select the scene you want to sketch, and then completely *forget* what you are drawing! The mind is an ingenious device: If you look at an object and *think* of what it is, you will probably impose onto your drawing some things that you know have to be there (every human hand has five fingers!) even

Illus. 52.

though they do not exist in the scene in front of you (the person's hand is turned so that only the thumb and two fingers are visible to you). So don't attempt to draw a "hand," a "chair," a "building," a "tree-lined street," or anything else that you could draw with your eyes closed (although the basic, "Brand X" images that emerge from your subconscious might resemble *Gramp's House* more than the building in front of you).

Instead of sketching "objects" in front of you, turn off your know-it-all mind and simply draw the outlines and shapes that appear in front of you just as though they represent a completely meaningless arrangement of lines. "This line runs from left to right. Then another line starts in the middle of that line and goes down at a 45° angle. Three horizontal lines run off this way. Then a half-circle over those lines. On the same height as the top of the half-circle, a long line ending in a triangle. At the top of the triangle, a long V-shape...."

After you have finished sketching, switch your mind back on and see what you have: "It's a building, with another building alongside of it. A large tree in the foreground dominates the scene. A sailboat in the background...." Or did all your meaningless lines and shapes produce something else: Perhaps a still-life scene on your dining room table? And everything is in correct perspective! Without your even thinking about it!

Several books can teach you all the fine points about sketching what you see by *not thinking* about what you are sketching. One of them is *Drawing on the Right Side of the Brain*, by Betty Edwards (Los Angeles: Jeremy P. Tarcher, 1979). Another is *The Natural Way to Draw*, by Kimon Nicolaides (Boston: Houghton Mifflin Co., 1941). But all the books go back to Cezanne's basis premise that everything to be painted consists of cubes, spheres, and cylinders. Often those cubes, spheres, and cylinders exist not only in real-life objects in front of your eyes but in "negative space." So the main point in sketching for braided cross-stitch is not to draw the *things* themselves, but the spaces and meaningless shapes all around them. It's very simple to master this trick, so get out there and sketch the scenes you want to reproduce in braided cross-stitch. Don't ask someone else to do it: That person won't know what it is about the scene that has appealed to you, and won't know what to include or omit. Because sketching for braided cross-stitch requires the selection of the scene, simplification by elimination of extraneous detail, and emphasis of the elements you want to retain. *You're* the needle artist! Don't ask someone else to make your design decisions for you. And don't settle for second-best, by saying, "I can't sketch this wonderful scene—I'll just buy a color postcard of the Washington Monument when I get back to the hotel."

Remember, as you are sketching, that the size of your sketch has no relationship whatsoever to the finished size of the piece that will be based on it: In order to produce a wall-size braided cross-stitch piece you do not have to draw a sketch, or a chart, that also is wall-size. The largest piece in this book, *Washington Mall with Triceratops,* is 10½ × 15 inches, but it was produced from a sketch that measures 5 × 8 inches, whereas the smaller *Beach House* (7 × 10 inches) is derived from a sketch measuring 6 × 9 inches. The reason why the sketches in Illus. 53 resulted in finished sizes having different proportions to one another is that *Beach House* was plotted onto 8-to-the-inch graph paper, *Bar Harbor* onto 10-to-the-inch graph paper, and *Washington Mall with Triceratops* was plotted onto 12-to-the-inch graph paper.

Illus. 53.

Illus. 53 (cont.).

After you have made your sketch, the rest of the procedure is exactly the same as with Method 2: Overlay various sizes of graph-paper grids until you get a size grid that accommodates your design with the detail that you want to render. Simply treat your own rough sketch as though it were a photograph, postcard, or drawing that you bought or saw in a magazine somewhere.

The pieces in this book that started life as rough scratchings on a piece of paper are as follows: *Bar Harbor, Beach House, Cat on TV, Four Birds* (except for *Fulmar Petrel*), *"Grandmother's Fan" Fan, Grey Skies Over the Golden Gate, Lilies of the Valley, New Orleans, Roses in Basket, Spring Flowers*, and *Washington Mall with Triceratops*.

Look around and see what appeals to you. Your church, town hall, a distinctive town feature, historic buildings, the place where you work or go to school, perhaps a favorite street scene? Look in your backyard: the bright yellow forsythia along the back fence, the grape hyacinths under them, the fresh green grass. All these scenes can be captured in braided cross-stitch for you and others to cherish for many years.

"But I don't have a backyard," you might say. Then look at the window box on your balcony, with the pink and salmon-colored impatiens tumbling out of it. Or look elsewhere; use your imagination! Your friend collects hippopotamuses. (Not real ones! Miniatures!) For years she has been looking unsuccessfully for a "hippo mother and child." Go to the library and get out a book on hippos. *There's* a photo of a hippo mother and child! Trace it onto plastic (you won't harm the library book) and reproduce the scene in braided cross-stitch. Give it to your friend for Christmas and be prepared to answer the question, "Where did you ever find it?" Then, "How did you ever do it?"

I know that you'll answer modestly and truthfully, "It was really very easy!"

▪ 5 ▪
Question and Answer Clinic

Q&A 1. The instructions in this book say to use Penelope (double-thread) canvas. The lady at my local yarn store says that "absolutely nobody" does any respectable needlework on Penelope canvas. She says that Penelope canvas is suitable only for children and rank beginners. She says that mono (single-thread) canvas can also be used with braided cross-stitch. Is she saying this only because mono canvas is the only kind she sells?

Probably. It's a shame that there's so much snobbery associated with needlework. It used to be the case, for example, that pieced quilts were associated with the "lower classes," who presumably had to make quilts out of scraps of fabric that had been magnanimously donated to them by the mistress after her ball gowns had been cut out. But appliqué quilts were presumably made by, and appreciated by, representatives of the "upper classes" who could afford to buy a bed-sized piece of fabric onto which one sewed large pieces of other expensive fabrics. Nowadays the distinction between pieced and appliqué quilts on the basis of the cost of the fabrics used is pretty much lost. The materials to make *any* kind of quilt are expensive.

In a similar manner, some types of embroidery and the materials to make them used to be associated with various social groups. Samplers used to be made by children, and often were executed entirely in cross-stitch. Moreover, many present-day projects intended for children or other beginning needleworkers include Penelope canvas and therefore are shunned by the "more discriminating" needleworker. It is true that cross-stitch, especially counted cross-stitch, has finally achieved the recognition that it deserves among American needleworkers, but that recognition was a long time coming!

In the meantime, however, the more "elegant" forms of needlework have required the use of mono canvas. Needlepoint reached its recent apogee on mono canvas. So did bargello. But the true reason why mono was associated with needlepoint and bargello is that the structure of each of those stitches demand single-thread canvas: If needlepoint or bargello is made on Penelope canvas, there are obvious unpleasant gaps between the stitches. So it is not *why* a piece of needlework is being made (for example, a piece of bargello to cover a Queen Anne chair in front of a manor house fireplace, as compared with a "God Bless This Mess" sampler to be given to Mom on Mother's Day) that determines the appropriate type of canvas, but, rather, the inherent nature of the stitch.

Thus, to come finally to the answer to the question: Penelope is required for braided cross-stitch because it creates a broad braid (Illus. 54). Mono

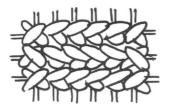

Illus. 54.

canvas creates a skinnier braid with spaces visible between the rows (Illus. 55). Using heavier yarns in an attempt to fill up these spaces results in a bulkier stitch that still does not have the typical braided appearance of this stitch.

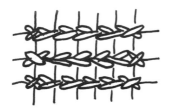

Illus. 55.

There is, however, a way in which mono (single-thread) canvas can be used for making braided cross-stitch: By treating the single threads as *sets* of 2, 3, or even more threads over which to make the stitch. But that would create a problem in selecting the mesh size of the canvas and establishing the correct balance between the amount of yarn used in the needle and the size of the stitches made on mono canvas in this way. Mono canvas with 10 mesh per inch, for example, would produce 5 stitches per inch if the stitches were worked over two canvas threads at a time; 12-mesh mono canvas worked over two canvas threads at a time would produce 6 stitches per inch—the same number of stitches per inch as produced on 6-mesh Penelope canvas—but the structure of the braided cross-stitch would be different from that on the 6-mesh Penelope canvas.

No, I think it would just be better for you to forget the idea of using mono canvas.

Q&A 2. Can't braided cross-stich be done on even-weave fabrics, rather than on canvas?

Yes, it can. Just as cross-stitch, and many other stitches, can be executed on a variety of materials with holes in them (cotton or linen canvas, plastic "canvas," punched paper, etc.), or on solid-woven fabrics with an irregular or a regular (even-weave) structure, braided cross-stitch can also be sewn directly onto woven fabrics (burlap, jute, linen, etc.) The Portuguese Arraiolos rugs are, in fact, made on a solid-woven rug backing. The few needlework books that describe "long-armed cross-stitch" usually show the stitch being made over "blocks" of threads of an even-weave fabric. But all the designs in this book were made on Penelope canvas and therefore I would recommend not using any even-weave fabrics for them: The final result might not be the one you desire or expect.

Q&A 3. You just said that "all the designs in this book were made on Penelope canvas," but isn't the Lilies of the Valley *made on "waste canvas"?*

"Waste canvas" is a type of double-thread canvas that is used when one wants to cross-stitch a design onto a fabric that cannot be marked or thread-counted. My wife, Gerry, for example, likes to select a flower or other motif from a print skirt and then, using waste canvas, cross-stitch that motif onto a black or other solid-color sweater or jersey to make a coordinated outfit. After the cross-stitch is completed over the intersections of the waste canvas, which were used as a guide for the placement of the stitches, the canvas is moistened and the canvas threads are pulled out, one by one, from embroidery, leaving only the cross-stitch yarns on the sweater or jersey. In *Lilies of the Valley*, I used waste canvas just as though it were ordinary Penelope canvas, but, obviously, did not remove the threads after the picture was finished. (If I did, there would only be a pile of little pieces of yarn on the floor!)

Q&A 4. Can interlock canvas or plastic canvas be used for the projects in this book?

In interlock canvas, the threads are woven in such a way as to twist around themselves to make the canvas less susceptible to being pulled out of shape during the stitching and also to prevent the threads from ravelling. Mono (single-thread) interlock is unsuitable for the projects in this book, just as regular mono canvas is unsuitable. Penelope (double-thread) interlock canvas can be used for these projects, but actually there is no need for its antidistortion capability, since there is never any distortion of the canvas when ordinary Penelope canvas is used for braided cross-stitch.

As for plastic canvas, it lacks the pliability of cotton Penelope canvas. Therefore, you cannot use the "like sewing" method (needle in and out, and pull the yarn through with a single motion) that makes braided cross-stitch so pleasant to do. Instead, plastic canvas invariably requires the use of the time-consuming and often awkward "stab stitch" method. Finally, when done on plastic, it has an appearance that is, for whatever reason, less appealing to me. Therefore, I prefer to use cotton Penelope canvas.

Q&A 5. The instructions say to cover the ends of the cut canvas with masking tape. Is that really necessary? Why can't I just leave the edges raw? Or maybe use the zigzag stitch on my sewing machine to prevent any ravelling?

It isn't just a matter of ravelling, although it sometimes does happen that raw edges of canvas will indeed ravel badly if the canvas is mishandled a lot. The purpose of the masking tape is to prevent the yarn from snagging on all those cut ends of threads as you work. It is very vexatious to be stitching placidly and to have the rhythm interrupted by having the yarn get caught on the edges of the canvas. So to preserve your tranquillity (a tranquillity that will be revealed in the evenness of your completed stitches), use the masking tape. But do not forget to remove it when the job is finished, and you want to block the piece and finish it for its final use—in a frame, as a pillow top, etc. Masking tape deteriorates over a period of years, and if you forget to remove it, it can discolor the canvas and adjacent yarns. You wouldn't want your beautiful work to be ruined fifty or a hundred years from now, would you?

Q&A 6. I can't seem to find three-ply woollen Persian-type yarns. But I can find three-ply synthetic

yarns. Can I use them instead? Or can I use any old yarn I have lying around the house—knitting yarns of wool or synthetic fibres—so long as they seem to fill in the holes of the canvas properly?

I wouldn't advise using synthetic Persian-type yarns. They lack the fluffiness (or "loft") of woollen yarns. Moreover, they're treacherous. If, for example, you decide to press your completed piece, using a steam iron with no pressure, a piece made with woollen yarns will look absolutely beautiful. But if you press a piece made with synthetic yarns, the life will often leave the piece: The stitches will flatten out completely. Why didn't you read the label first?—"Use cool iron only!" Or can you be absolutely certain that your synthetic yarns will never feel any heat? Even fifty years from now?

As for using knitting yarns, whether made of wool or synthetic fibres, I wouldn't advise that either. Knitting yarns are made of softer fibres than embroidery yarns. Hence they are more likely to break or become thin from being pulled through the canvas. Also, they are more likely to "pill" or become soiled when subjected to use (as in a pillow top).

I'd advise you to keep looking, even if you have to wait a few more days to start your first project. Don't be so anxious to start any needlework that you use the wrong materials, which will only disappoint you in the end instead of making you want to continue in that medium.

Q&A 7. I bought some of that three-ply woollen Persian-type yarn and took it home. Then I separated one strand of it into three individual plies as you said to do. But each of those individual plies is itself made up of two thinner plies of yarn. Am I supposed to separate the three individual plies into these thinner ones?

I was afraid that someone was going to look at one of those three individual plies under a magnifying glass!

To understand the structure of woollen yarns, you have to know that individual fibres of wool, when spun together, hook into one another to form yarns. The longer the fibres and the tighter the twisting, the stronger the yarns will be. In making three-ply Persian-type yarns, long, soft, and relatively weak fibres are first spun into thin yarns. Two of the single yarns are then spun together to form what becomes a single ply of the three-ply yarn. The soft fibres of the two thin yarns lock together to form a very strong yarn that is difficult to separate into the two original yarns. One wouldn't want to do that anyway, because one would be going back to the relatively weaker yarns.

When three of these single plies (each of which actually consists of two thinner ones, as you discovered) are spun together loosely, they form a three-ply yarn that can indeed be separated easily into the three component plies. And that's what you're supposed to do: separate the three-ply yarns into three individual plies, then put two of those individual plies, either two of the same color, or one each of two different colors, into your needle.

Q&A 8. How much yarn of each color should I buy?

As I explained in chapter 3, there are many variables that can affect the amounts of yarn required, so I can only reiterate that you should buy more of a color than you think you need. Many of the designs in this book require only small amounts of certain colors—certainly no more than one or two strands as purchased in a yarn shop that sells individual strands of three-ply Persian-type yarns.

But for designs that require large amounts of only a few colors, there is a way for you to estimate your yarn requirements. Take a sample strand of the three-ply yarn as purchased in your local yarn shop or other source. Separate it into three individual plies of yarn. Put two plies back together, thread a tapestry needle, and see how many braided cross-stitches you can make on the type of canvas that you plan to use. Then take the third ply of that sample strand. Cut it in half to get two shorter pieces and put both pieces into the needle. See how many stitches you can make with that needleful. Add the two totals together and that is how many stitches you can make from one purchased strand of three-ply yarn. If the total number of stitches in a particular color is, say, 300, divide the 300 by the total number of stitches per strand. That is the approximate number of strands you have to buy. But if the total number of stitches in a particular two-color blend is 300, divide the 300 by the total number of stitches per strand. Then take half the number

of the result for the first color, and half for the second color.

But why bother with all these calculations? It's more fun to "guess high," and have all that left-over yarn to play with later on.

Q&A 9. How long a piece of yarn should I put in the needle?

Everyone's arm is of a different length, so the rule is "Start with a piece of yarn that enables you to pull the yarn through the canvas in a single uninterrupted motion." If the yarn is too long, the yarn doesn't come all the way through the canvas, and you have to pull it a second time. This not only breaks your stitching rhythm, but also results in a very uneven texture in the final stitches. So start with a comfortable length that enables you to complete each stitch easily, without handling or tugging at the yarn. After a few stitches, the yarn will get shorter anyway, but anything that allows you to stitch smoothly and evenly, without the frustration of interrupting the methodological "zip! zip! zip!" of the needle, should be encouraged.

Q&A 10. What type of needle should I use? And what difference does the size make?

You should always use a tapestry needle, which has a blunt point. A needle with a sharp point can pierce the canvas threads, breaking them in the middle of a stitch or weakening them so that they break soon thereafter. Since there are holes in the canvas, there is no need for the piercing action of a sharp needle. As for the size of the tapestry needle, it can be any size that feels comfortable to you, so long as you can thread it easily with the two plies of the Persian yarn. But it should not be so large that the needle and the yarn in it distort the canvas threads while you are making the stitches. The size of the needle is not as critical in braided cross-stitch as it is in needlepoint, where the slight distortion of the canvas threads as each stitch is made can result in horrendous distortion of the completed work, which distortion cannot be removed by any amount of blocking or reblocking.

The size of tapestry needle that I prefer is #20. But sizes in needles are by no means standard. Size 20 needles may vary from manufacturer to manufacturer, and even from batch to batch. I have some #20 needles that are a bit heftier and a bit nicer to use than others: Why can't I find more of them, instead of having to keep buying newer and newer supplies of needles and testing them like Goldilocks' testing porridge? Once you find the size and manufacturer of needle that are your favorites, buy lots of needles, so that you'll never feel the need to use a needle that you're uncomfortable with.

Q&A 11. Why do I need a lot of needles? Can't I make the whole piece with a single needle?

Sure you can, but if you are working on a piece that has, say, 10 different color combinations, it can be very time-consuming to make a few stitches of color A, take the yarn out of the needle, rethread the needle with color Q and make a few stitches, unthread the needle, load it with color Z and make a few stitches, then, what? Color A again! It's much easier to keep a needle loaded with each color. Then you pick up the needle with color A, make the stitches, secure the yarn on the back of the canvas, cut off the end of the yarn, and put the needle down until you need that color again. Then simply pick up an already loaded needle with the next color and make the stitches in that color. After fastening off and cutting that yarn, lay that needle down and pick up the next one you need.

Use whatever system you like to keep the needlefuls in order, so that you don't have to go searching. "Where's that needleful of color A that I had a minute ago?" A system I like to use is just to have a piece of paper into which I stick the loaded needle after I have finished making the stitches with it (Illus. 56). I also like to keep small quantities of the yarns for each color combination in small paper cups on which I indicate

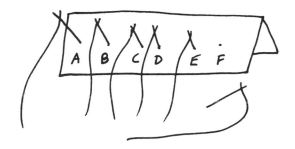

Illus. 56.

with a marking pen the color code and the color numbers (Illus. 57). That way I do not have to search for a particular color when I need it.

Illus. 57.

Q&A 12. If I've got all these needles loaded with different color combinations, why don't I do an entire row of the design at a time, dangling the various needles down the back like bobbins in knitting Argyle socks? That way I could make two stitches of red, then three stitches of blue, then one stitch of black, then two stitches of red, then....

Take my advice. Don't do it that way! If you do, you'll have to keep referring *constantly* to the chart, and you will find the process very time-consuming, if not mentally shattering. The easy way to do braided cross-stitch is to look briefly at the chart, memorize the shape of the area to make in a particular color, and then construct it on the canvas. If it's a square of four rows of four stitches of color M, then make that entire square at one time and cut the yarn loose. It's like paint-by-numbers, or "color-inside-the-lines" as you used to do in kindergarten. Then look at the chart, see that the next shape is a rectangle of four rows of six stitches of color Q, and do *that* area. Use your memory to eliminate the tedium of referring to the chart excessively.

But breaking away from the chart is not the only reason why I advise against using the Argyle bobbin method. I've seen the results of braided cross-stitch done by this method and they look like the rocky road to Dublin. I don't mean the quilt design called *Rocky Road to Dublin*. I mean the rocky road (with rocks!) to Dublin. The constant discarding and picking up of the various needles breaks the even rhythm of stitch-making that develops when you work an area of color at a time. As the rhythm keeps changing jerkily, the poor tortured stitches show it. It's not syncopated rhythm. It's cacophony.

Q&A 13. Okay, I've got my needles loaded up with the various colors of yarns and I'm ready to go. But I just can't read that chart! Why can't I get pictures painted on canvas and do braided cross-stitch that way, the way I can get painted canvas that I do needlepoint on?

Don't get me started on the argument of which is "easiest," printed charts on paper that are used to create needlework on a blank piece of canvas or fabric, or designs that are printed "right there" on the canvas or fabric itself. It's like the argument between people who love raw oysters and those who hate them. But I will say one thing: People who have finally taken the plunge and gotten involved with counted cross-stitch will all testify that it is easier to get a precisely made set of crosses by looking at a chart and then counting the appropriate number of threads on a piece of canvas or even-weave cloth than it is to cover over a series of crosses that have been printed slightly askew onto canvas or unevenly-woven cloth. And color subtleties are much easier to reproduce when you see in a chart a configuration like this:

$$+ + + +$$
$$+ + : +$$
$$+ : : +$$

and the cross-stitched picture includes an area of the cutest angel's face in which the cheek is mostly color +, but the accent of orange pink represented by : highlights the cheek in exactly the right place.

So take my word. Printed charts enable you to put one stitch or a lot of stitches of *exactly* the right color in *exactly* the right place.

Q&A 14. But the charts are so small! I have trouble seeing all those little symbols. Is there anything I can do to improve the situation?

Sure. Go to a copy store and have them make an *enlarged* xerographic copy of the chart. It will only cost a few cents, but it will be money well spent. Obviously, there is a limitation to the size of the charts that can be printed in any needlework book or magazine. The charts in this book started out large and had to be reduced to fit onto the pages of the book. All you're doing is bringing them up to their original size again.

When you get a xerographic copy of the chart, whether it is enlarged or the same size, you can hand-color it to make it easier to read. To keep the costs of printing this book down, the charts are not in color. But there is no reason why you can't color the charts to make them easier to read, using water colors, colored pencils, and so forth, color the sky blue (or three shades of blue if necessary), color the grass green (or four shades of green if necessary). You wouldn't want to do that in the book itself, but you can do it easily on your disposable xerographic copy.

Q&A 15. But I don't have three shades of blue pencils or four shades of green. How do I differentiate among the various colors on the diagram?

Who says you have to use blue to represent blue, or green to represent green? You can use any colors that you like, selecting them completely arbitrarily, so that each color you use represents a different color combination. Use purple to color every area of color A (whether color A represents a blend of sky-blue colors or a blend of grass-green colors); use red to color every area of color B (whether it represents red or it *doesn't* represent red). In a very short time you will memorize your own arbitrary codings. Whenever you see purple on your hand-colored chart, you will automatically reach for the needle with the sky-blue color combination, or whatever.

Q&A 16. I've studied and studied the chart, but I still can't understand how to make those four squares of color A A A A fit into four holes in the canvas. I feel so dumb! What am I doing wrong?

Actually this isn't a dumb question, but it deals with a problem that is often overlooked by experienced needleworkers who use charts. People who have been doing cross-stitch for a long time know that, when they look at a chart, the symbols A A A A refer to four stitches that are constructed over canvas *threads*. The symbols don't have anything to do with the *holes* on the canvas. You can't *fit* a single stitch of any kind in a hole!

Many years ago, teaching a course on cross-stitch, I asked the students a seemingly unrelated question, "How much dirt is in a hole one foot square and one foot deep?" After getting all kinds of answers, I said, "There's *no* dirt in a hole; it's all been taken out!" Then, holding up a piece of canvas, I asked, "How many cross-stitches can you get in a single hole of this canvas?"

Once again I got all kinds of answers. "One!" "Ten!" "As many as you want!"

"No," I answered, "it's the same answer; you can't get *any* cross-stitches in one hole. It takes *four holes* to make a cross-stitch!"

That's right! If a diagram represents a single cross-stitch (or a single *tvistsöm* stitch) by a single symbol—for example, A—that means that the actual stitch will cover one *intersection*, but will occupy four holes (Illus. 58).

Illus. 58.

Similarly, A A A A will cover four intersections, and no one really cares about how many holes are involved. The experienced needleworker assumes that everyone knows that the chart refers to the stitches. But the beginning needleworker sometimes has to learn to stop thinking about holes. Don't *think* of holes! Don't count the holes! Don't even *say* holes! Instead, think and say "10-mesh canvas" or "canvas 10 intersections to the inch." Eventually you too will learn to read charts as stitches.

Q&A 17. I know that I'm supposed to glance occasionally at the chart and memorize the shape of the areas of color I'm supposed to make. But I find it hard to do that. I keep looking at the chart to make one or two stitches, then back again to make two or three more. What am I doing wrong?

You should try to assign some kind of name—no matter how silly it sounds to anyone else. Here are a few examples of how I would memorize a shape and then make the stitches on the canvas without looking back at the chart again until the shape is finished. (Illus. 59).

A. Block of five A's.

B. Square of five B's; center of K.

C. I with five C's on top, bottom, and stem; fill-in on left with L, with M on right.

Illus. 59.

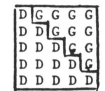

D. Right triangle, flush on left, 1 to 5 stitches of D; fill-in with G.

E. Upside-down L of 5 Y's on each side; fill-in with up-and-down S.

These descriptions may sound elaborate now, because they had to be verbalized to make *my* system intelligible to *you*. But as you devise your own names for the areas of color, you will recognize the shapes on the chart more and more quickly and translate them into stitches on canvas with fewer and fewer glances at the chart.

Q&A 18. All this theorizing is very nice, but I can't even get my needle threaded yet. Is there an easy way to do it?

One way that needleworkers thread the needle (instead of licking the cut end of the yarn and trying to push the pieces of moist, fuzzy "spaghetti" into the eye of the needle) is to make a loop of the yarn around the needle and pull the loop tight (Illus. 60). Then pinch the yarn tightly

Illus.60.

Illus. 63.

close to the top of the loop (Illus. 61). Then slide the loop off the needle and, still pinching it tightly, squeeze it through the eye of the needle.

Illus. 61.

Another method is even easier, but it requires a strip of paper that is narrow enough to be doubled and still fit through the eye of the tapestry needle you are using. Cut a narrow strip of paper, fold it in half, and insert the folded end through the eye of the needle (Illus. 62). Insert the cut

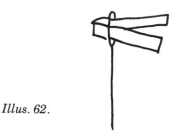

Illus. 62.

end or ends of the yarn between the open ends of the strip (Illus. 63). Pinch everything tightly and push the strip of paper the rest of the way through the hole, taking the yarn with it.

Q&A 19. The instructions in chapter 2, "Making a Practice Piece," say to leave a "tail" whenever starting a new piece of canvas, and to cover it with subsequent stitches. Or to fasten a new piece of yarn by leaving the tail under the backside of completed stitches, and then bringing the needle up to the top of the canvas. A friend of mine says that I should leave the tail on top of the canvas, and cover it with stitches on the top, so that the back of the canvas is "perfectly neat." What do you think about that?

Portuguese rugs made with braided cross-stitch (Arraiolos rugs) are indeed made with the beginning and ending "tails" of the yarn left on the top of the rug. This presumably improves the wear properties of the rug, since it provides more wool on the surface that takes the force of the footsteps. But, probably more importantly, the backside of the rug is left neat so that the hostess will not be embarrassed when a visiting needle-worker turns back the rug to inspect the back of the rug. There are, as you know, many people who say, "I was told that the back of needlework should always be as neat as the front." Presumably the visiting needleworker would be inclined, upon seeing a covered-up "tail" of yarn on the underside of the rug, to say, "Oh dear, that's not very neat, is it?"

Personally, I used to worry, many years ago, about whether the back of my cross-stitch, nee-dlepoint, braided cross-stitch, hand-woven tapes-try, and so forth was as "neat as the front." Then

106

I read in a book on tapestry weaving that it was always traditional in the weaving of Gobelin tapestries, and continues to be traditional, to leave long tails of the tapestry yarns hanging from the back of the tapestry. This was done not only to ensure that the woven areas of color would not pop out to the front side of the tapestry, but also "to provide a cushion of air between the tapestry and the cold castle walls on which it was hung." The tails were left for the sake of insulation! (They didn't have Fiberglass back then in the days of chivalry.)

Nowadays, when one peeks carefully behind the Gobelin tapestries hanging on museum walls (one is definitely not allowed to touch them with the hands, so make sure that the guard realizes that you are only peeking!), one can see that the entire back of the tapestry has been covered with a piece of fabric that covers over all those unsightly ends of yarn. Well, then, whenever I worry, for however fleeting a split second, about whether the back of my needlework looks neat, I always reassure myself by saying, "I'm doing it in the Gobelin manner!"

When the braided cross-stitch piece is completed, it is put into a frame, made into a pillow top, or otherwise finished in a way that conceals the underneath part of the canvas. So my advice to you is to strive to make the top side as neat as possible (and this includes beginning and ending the yarns on the back), and not to worry one iota about what the back looks like.

Q&A 20. The instructions for making the practice piece say to start close to the top of the canvas and then work downwards. Wouldn't it be easier to start somewhere else in the chart? Maybe at the bottommost row? Or in the center?

One of the nice features of braided cross-stitch is that the needleworker actually can start just about anywhere he or she wants to. As you become more experienced, you will be able to decide, when working different projects, where you want to begin. Sometimes, especially with a complicated design, I begin in the exact center of the design. To do this, I locate the exact center of the canvas (by folding the canvas once crosswise, then folding it again in the other direction; then marking the center intersection on the canvas).

Then I work the area of color that includes the center intersection and keep working outward until I reach the outer edges.

In other instance it is easier to work the design row-by-row. But should those rows be made from top to bottom of the canvas? Or from bottom to top? There are a couple of reasons why I prefer to make the rows from bottom to top. First, it is easier to poke the needle down into an already completed stitch and then up into an open hole (Illus. 64) than it is to poke the needle down into an

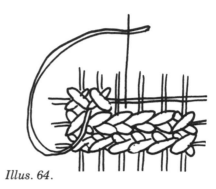

Illus. 64.

open hole and then up through an already completed stitch, while making sure that the needle does not split or otherwise interfere with that completed stitch (Illus. 65).

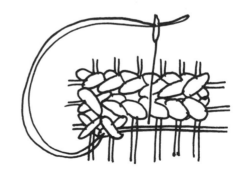

Illus. 65.

Secondly, each row of stitches always begins by bringing the needle up at the bottom-left of a regular row (or the bottom-right of a return row), and always ends by inserting the needle in the upper-right corner of a regular row (or upper-left corner of a return row). If one works from the bottom to the top of the canvas, one often encounters situations in which the "down" location of one stitch coincides with the "up" location of the stitch above it. If you pull the yarn down through that hole, the next stitch will bring it back up again (Illus. 66). Of course the problem is not insurmountable; resolve it by "fudging" the first stitch or two of each ensuing row, but I think it's easier simply to avoid the problem by always working the rows from the top of the canvas.

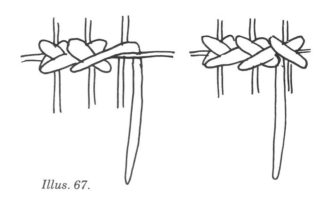

Illus. 67.

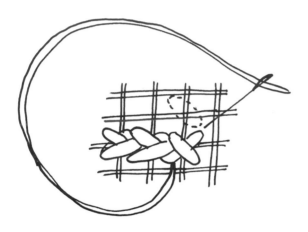

Illus. 66.

Q&A 21. I seem to be like the kid who failed in the spelling bee with the word "banana." ("I know how to begin it but I don't know how to end it!") I know how to do braided cross-stitch, but if the phone rings and I'm interrupted, or if I'm coming to the end of a piece of yarn, I don't know how to end it. Then when I begin making more stitches, the stitches don't look right. What can I do to resolve this problem?

First, you have to be able to look at a row of stitches that has been interrupted and tell whether the last stitch has been only half-completed (by going forward to empty holes) or has been *completed* (by going back to the previous set of holes). That's easy to tell, once you are aware of what you're looking for. Illus. 67 shows what a half-completed stitch and a complete stitch look like in a regular row, and Illus. 68 shows what a

half-completed and a complete stitch look like in a return row. In both kinds of rows, note that the unworked yarn emerges from the bottom of the completed stitch.

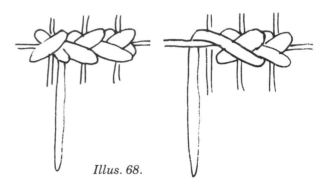

Illus. 68.

Whenever you are interrupted by the phone, or otherwise want to stop, get in the habit of leaving a stitch half-completed: it is easier to recognize, since the yarn has been brought forward to empty holes.

Also, when coming to the end of a piece of yarn, it is easier to insert the needle at the top of the forward half of the stitch and to bring the yarn to the back and fasten it off under some completed stitches (Illus. 69). Fasten on the new

Illus. 69. Insert needle; bring yarn to back and fasten off.

108

yarn, and bring it up at the bottom of the forward half of the stitch and resume stitching by going back and completing the stitch (Illus. 70).

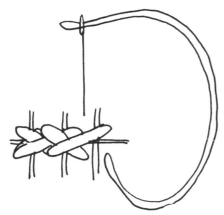

Illus. 70. Fasten new yarn on back; bring needle up to front. "Go back" to resume stitching.

Q&A 22. As I was stitching, I made three extra stitches of one color. I tried to take them out by inserting the needle back into the canvas and I created a terrible mess. What did I do wrong?

The thing you did wrong was to try to sew yourself out of a bad situation. By inserting the needle back into the canvas, you got the yarn entangled in the stitches you had made. The trick in removing stitches is to unthread the needle immediately! Then, pull on the yarn until it comes out of the hole. Keep repeating this process, pulling the yarn out of the holes until the "head" appears again, and you have removed the extra stitches. Now rethread the needle and fasten the yarn off on the back of the work, or put additional stitches in where they were supposed to go.

Q&A 23. I didn't notice that I had made a mistake until after I had put in a lot of other stitches. What should I do now?

Well, if it's a matter of only one wrong stitch you might want to just leave it there but do what I do: Cover it up with another stitch of the correct color. It's amazing how, in braided cross-stitch, one stitch covered up by another one won't be discernible at all in the finished piece. You may have to pull the yarn a bit more tightly to pack the stitch down, but usually even that is unnecessary to conceal an incorrect stitch.

If it's a matter of two or more wrong stitches, however, I'm afraid that you'll just have to remove them. To do that, cut away the wrong stitches *very carefully* by inserting the tips of sharp-pointed embroidery scissors under the topmost loop of yarn in each stitch and cutting that loop only. Don't try to cut through the entire stitch, or you may cut too far down and cut one of the threads in the canvas! After the top loops of all the incorrect stitches have been cut, pick away the pieces of yarn with the point of your needle and your fingers. If possible, remove a couple of the correct stitches also, so that you can put them back in with a fresh piece of yarn and fasten off that piece of yarn on the back. If you remove only the incorrect stitches, the cut end of the adjacent correct one might otherwise work itself to the top of the canvas.

Q&A 24. You won't believe this, but, despite all my caution in cutting away some incorrect stitches, I must have accidentally cut some of the canvas threads! Now what do I do?

No problem! If the cut thread is in an area of mostly unworked canvas, just sew on a patch of canvas (for "how-to," see *Q&A 25*) and work the stitches through the two layers of canvas: the canvas with the cut threads and the canvas patch.

If the cut canvas threads are in a small area that is surrounded by worked stitches and that is too small for sewing on a patch of canvas, create a latticework of hand-sewn threads to duplicate all the visible canvas threads (including the cut threads). Thread an ordinary sewing needle with strong thread (such as quilting thread). Fasten the end of the thread to some of the completed work on the back; then sew back and forth, as though darning the hole in a sock (does anyone do that nowadays?), running the thread along one pair of canvas threads, into a worked area for fastening, then back along another pair of canvas threads. Repeat this process until the supporting "lattice" is complete. Now turn the canvas to the front again and make the necessary stitches over the canvas threads and the reinforcing threads that you have just sewn. The area will be stronger than the rest of the canvas and there will be no sign of what you thought was a calamity.

Q&A 25. The Penelope canvas that I bought at the yarn store must have had a broken thread in it, but I didn't notice it until I got home. Can I use the canvas?

Whenever you buy canvas, make sure that there are no breaks in it, or any knots in the canvas threads (which might break at some time in the future). But occasionally you might encounter a previously unnoticed break in canvas threads in a piece of canvas that you are planning to use. Or maybe, after carefully cutting a piece of canvas to the correct size for your future project, you have dropped the scissors right down onto the canvas, cutting a pair of threads. Or do these things happen only to me?

The easy way out would be to discard the canvas for the project originally planned, and to cut it into smaller pieces for other, less ambitious projects. But what if this is the only piece of canvas you have, and you absolutely must repair it and use it? In that case, cut a patch, approximately 2″ square, of the same kind of canvas (the same number of intersections per inch) and, using ordinary sewing thread, whipstitch it to the backside of the canvas in such a way that the center of the patch is directly under the broken canvas threads and all the threads in the canvas are directly superimposed on the threads in the path (Illus. 71, view from back). If all the threads

do not line up perfectly, it may be that your canvas is not exactly even-weave: the number of threads per inch in one direction may be slightly different from the number in the other direction. In that instance, turn the patch until the threads do coincide, and then whipstitch the patch down.

Start making the braided cross-stitch on the canvas as though nothing happened. When you reach the patched area, simply make the stitches through the two layers of canvas—the large piece and the patch. Do this in the entire 2″-square area that has the patch, and the completed work will not show in any way that that area had been repaired. True, little wispy ends of canvas threads from the patch will probably stick out on the back of the canvas, since there is not enough yarn on the underneath part to cover them completely. But who's going to scrutinize the back of your piece that critically, anyway?

Q&A 26. An interior decorator friend tells me that the only people in Portugal who use the Arraiolos stitch are women prisoners who make rugs while they're serving out their sentence. Can that be true?

It used to be true that, in previous unhappy days in Portugal, there were a lot of women serving long terms in prison, and it was true that many of those women did produce Portuguese needlepoint rugs (that is, rugs made with the Arraiolos stitch) for sale throughout the world. Nowadays, however, in the more liberal political atmosphere in Portugal, there are fewer women in prisons who are serving long terms. Therefore, special orders for rugs made in Portuguese prisons take longer to be completed, and the rugs themselves are more expensive than they used to be in what was for interior decorators, if not for the general Portuguese population, "the good old days."

As for any needleworkers other than prisoners who use the Arraiolos stitch in Portugal, I'll check that out on my next (and first) trip to Portugal, and report back to you in my next book.

Q&A 27. A needleworker friend of mine says that braided cross-stitch should actually be called the knitting stitch, because it looks like knitting. She also says that, when making the rows of stitches from left to right, I shouldn't point the needle perpendicularly to the rows of stitches (that is, point

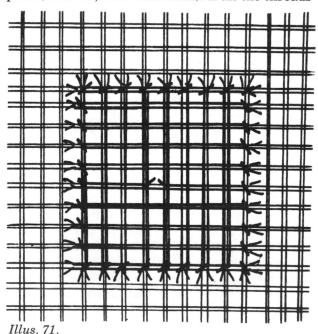

Illus. 71.

the needle directly at me), but should make a series of backstitches on the canvas (that is, always point the needle to the right). Who's confused?

A *lot* of people are confused about what braided cross-stitch is and what it isn't. First, it does somewhat resemble knitting, but it is not the "knitting stitch" encountered in ordinary canvas embroidery. That name is applied to what is simply two alternating rows of slanting Gobelin stitches (Illus. 72), usually worked on mono (rather than Penelope) canvas.

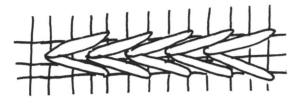

Illus. 72.

Another canvas-embroidery stitch that is called the knit stitch is made over three rows of mono canvas. To make this stitch, one makes a series of long slanting Gobelin stitches from left to right; then one makes a series of equally long slanting Gobelin stitches back over the first series of stitches, weaving the needle over and under those previous stitches (Illus. 73). The braid that is visible on the surface of the canvas looks almost the same as braided cross-stitch, but is obviously more suitable for working in entire rows, rather than as individual stitches. Even when worked in rows, it is a difficult stitch, requiring constant counting of threads to make sure that the over-and-under weaving is done correctly.

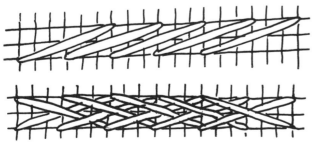

Illus. 73.

Neither the "knitting stitch" nor the "knit stitch" of canvas embroidery contains any cross-stitches at all. Both stitches also lack the typical feature of braided cross-stitch (the presence of a long journey of yarn to begin the cross-stitch and a short journey to complete it). And, finally, they lack the sparse look on the backside of the canvas, since the backside of knitting stitch and knit stitch reveals a thick padding of the underneath half of each Gobelin stitch.

What about making braided cross-stitch by making a series of backstitches, instead of pointing the needle perpendicular to the row of stitches you are making? Well, the stitch that results is close to, but not the same as, braided cross-stitch, even though some needlepoint books say that this stitch is the same. But it is obvious from Illus. 74 that this stitch does not create a braid, but a series of overlapping lopsided crosses. The stitch (which produces two lines of

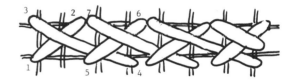

Illus. 74.

horizontal stitches on the backside of the canvas —Illus. 75), can be made in one direction only; the canvas must be inverted in order to make a return row.

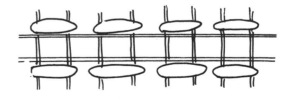

Illus. 75.

I hope I don't sound like a nitpicker about what braided cross-stitch is and what it is not, but in this age of specialization it seems imperative to know one's medium completely—not only its artistic capabilities, but also the features that make it distinctive, differentiating it from other media. Have you found, as I have, that in this age of specialization the experts sometimes do not know their subject well? Have you ever taken your car to a place that specializes in installing shock absorbers and found out a couple of thousand unsatisfactory miles later that the shock absorbers had been installed upside down? If so, you are probably not surprised that there has been some confusion, even on the part of some needlepoint experts (present company excepted!), about how to make the braided cross-stitch. Would you, thus, be surprised to see photographs and diagrams in needlepoint books showing rows of braided cross-stitches made as shown in Illus. 76?

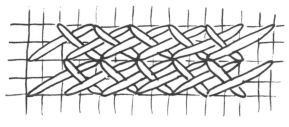

Illus. 76.

Q&A 28. I find it awkward to poke the needle into the canvas perpendicular to the rows of stitches. I keep thinking I'm going to stick the needle into my chest! Isn't there an easier way to do it?

Yes, there is. Now that you are an expert with the stitch, always going forward to empty holes, and then going back to complete the stitch, and are aware that the needle is always perpendicular to the stitches that you are making, it's time to introduce you to the "roll-'em-up" technique.

To do a regular row, for example, the top row of your piece, roll up the canvas and hold the cylinder of canvas in your left hand (Illus. 77). Now the top row of the piece will be at the open, right-hand edge of the canvas. Make the stitches in the usual way: by bringing the yarn up from the back; going forward (that is, *down*) to empty holes; going back (that is, *up*) to the half-stitch just made; then forward (down) again. By continuing in this manner, you always insert the needle in the correct relationship to the stitches, but the needle always points right to left. This really *is* like sewing, and there is no chance in the

world that you're going to stick yourself in the chest.

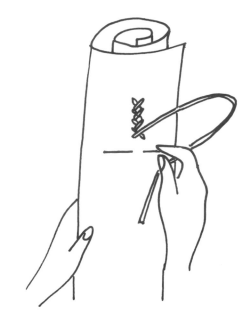

Illus. 77.

When you finish the first row and you want to make a return row, there is no need to unroll the canvas or change its position. Simply bring the yarn up to the top of the canvas; go forward (that is, *up*) to empty holes; go back (that is, *down*) to complete the stitch; continue going forward and back as you complete the row of stitches in the return row. You are still inserting the needle as in sewing, from right to left. When you unroll the canvas and turn it back to its original position, the two rows you just made will look absolutely correct as two horizontal rows of stitches, and will look as though you had made them by the usual needle-at-the-chest method.

Q&A 29. The directions for a few of the designs in this book include references to "mistakes" that are also shown on the charts. If you knew you had made mistakes, why didn't you correct them, instead of printing them?

These are deliberate mistakes that are typical of many quilters and other types of handwork, not only in this country but presumably in most cultures. When you inspect an Oriental rug and see that most of the red diamonds have orange centers, but one red diamond has a green center, do you tell yourself, *The rug-weaver made a mistake there!* Or rationalize, *He must have run out of orange?* Or, when you look closely at an Amish quilt and see that most of the nine-patch blocks consist of five dark blue and four light blue squares, but one block consists of *four* dark blue and *five* light blue, do you similarly think that the quilter made a mistake accidentally? Or if all the blocks in that quilt are dark blue and light blue, except for one block that is dark *green* and light blue, do you think that the quilter, like the rug-weaver, ran out of a certain color and had to make do?

Well, maybe the rug-weaver and the Amish quilter goofed, but it is more probable that they made those mistakes deliberately. Especially since they jump right out, even to the casual observer. *But why would they do that and spoil a perfect design?* you might ask. One theory is that for thousands of years, handcraftsmen in all societies have incorporated some kind of mistake in each piece they made, in order to convince the Almighty that they were aware that only the Almighty could make a truly perfect creation and the handcraftsman, however talented he or she was, was not presuming to claim that degree of perfection. Nowadays the habit persists among craftsmen, not as a superstition (*If I don't put in a deliberate mistake, I might lose my inspiration*), but just as a whimsical variation.

Several years ago I went to an exhibition of Indian pottery, where I read an exhibit sign pointing out that the painted circle at the top of each pot was left open, "in order for the Spirit of the Clay to enter and leave the pot at will." A week or so afterwards, I attended the annual American Folklife Festival on the Mall in Washington, D.C., and happened to stop in front of the exhibit where some Pima Indians from California were making and displaying baskets. The baskets looked absolutely perfect. So I asked one of the ladies making them whether she, like Indian potters, ever left any of the circles unclosed, or if she ever incorporated a "mistake" in her baskets deliberately. "No," she said, "I never make any mistakes deliberately, but I do pull a hair out of my head and weave it into each basket I make." That sounded to me like the kind of mistake that only Someone Special would notice!

In this age of regimentation, when the state government tells you whether you will or will not put a child's car seat in your car or whether you will use your seat belt, it's nice to have a psychological release at times. I know that I have to stay within the lines of social behavior and not drive through a red light. But I don't really have to stay within the lines when I'm making a pen-and-ink sketch and coloring in the areas with soft-tipped pens. Similarly, whenever I do any kind of needlework, I often incorporate some "mistake" in it, just as Victor Borge, for whatever *his* reasons are, hits an obvious clinker in the middle of a piano piece that we Borge fans may have been listening to too seriously.

Maybe that's the key. Some people, who are to my mind too serious, say of others who put a mistake in their quilts, "That is the height of arrogance! It states that the maker could actually have made a perfect quilt if she had wanted to, but she deigned not to." Whenever I put a "clinker" in any of my pieces, I am not that presumptuous. I *think* I'm doing it in fun. I don't try to hide my mistakes, intentional or otherwise.

If you don't want to join in the fun (because you are striving for perfection, or for whatever reason), then by all means correct these egregious errors. But I'm warning you: I've sneaked other "mistakes" into certain designs without labelling them. But I'm not so mischievous that I won't give you this hint: It is sort of traditional to put the "mistake" in the lower right-hand corner of a quilt, where everyone can see it.

If you find any unintentional mistakes in this book—maybe I have transposed the order number of yarns, so that something that should be light blue turns out to be bright purple—I hope you forgive me. I would appreciate your informing me of that kind of *real* mistake so that I can take steps to correct it, and your giving me proof, once again, that I'm only human.

Q&A 30. I'm left-handed. Are there are special instructions that I have to follow in order to do braided cross-stitch?

No, indeed! Braided cross-stitch is extremely easy for left-handers to assimilate. Moreover, the final results are completely indistinguishable from those achieved by right-handers. As a left-hander, you have probably read books on needlepoint that tell you it is perfectly all right for you to make all the stitches in continental stitch slant from lower right to upper left (like the first stroke of a capital V), instead of the "right" way to do continental stitch (all stitches slanting like the *second* stroke of a capital V). But you and I know that if you actually made continental stitch, or counted cross-stitch, or many other stitches, with the yarn slanting in other than the "right" direction, you'd have plenty of experts pointing out your cardinal sin to you.

With braided cross-stitch the experts will never know that the piece was made by a leftie! All you have to do is to reverse all the directions in this book. You don't even have to hold a mirror up to the pages, or hold the pages up against the light and have the diagrams shine through from the reverse side. All you have to do is remember that you start on the right-hand edge of the row and make the stitches from right to left: Bringing the needle up at the beginning of the row, going forward (to your left) to empty holes, then going back (to your right) to holes already worked. And the return row, for you, is made by constructing the rows of stitches from left to right: Bringing the needle up at the beginning of the row, going forward (to your right) to empty holes, then going back (to your left).

Q&A 31. I went to the yarn store and bought the colors of Paternayan three-ply yarns that are indicated in the directions. But the colors of the completed piece don't look exactly like the colors in the photograph in the book. What's wrong?

Color is a very complicated concept. The human eye can distinguish among hundreds of thousands of different colors. There are very complicated theories of color and very detailed books on color, both for the theoretician and for the ordinary craftsperson. Since this book is primarily one that tells you, the needleworker, how to reproduce the pieces I designed, I have not included any detailed discussion of color such as I would have included in a book on braided cross-stitch design proper.

But even in reproducing colors, one encounters difficulties. The problem is that yarns start out, in the case of wool, on an animal's back. The animal's wool is, let's say for the sake of simplicity, white. After the wool is cleaned and otherwise prepared, it is dyed. Natural dyes, those derived from plant leaves, roots, etc., have the many variations that give hand-dyed yarns their subtle effect. But, obviously, one batch of natural dyes will always differ from another—the lily-of-the-valley leaves that are picked in the early spring produce a dye that is different than one produced from the leaves that are picked in the late summer, and this year's batch is different because this year was especially rainy. Even commercially produced dyes, such as the ones used to produce needlework yarns, can vary from batch to batch. Hence the need to check the dye-lot numbers when making a large area of a solid color.

And so, the dyes used in the wool yarns can vary. When one takes a photograph of anything the colors in the photograph may appear a little bit off: The dyes in the photographic film react differently from situation to situation, from manufacturer to manufacturer, from film type to film type.

And when photographs, such as the ones appearing in this book, are subjected to the color-separation process in order to be printed, the situation is more complicated than just passing a few photographs around the room. The components of each color in the photograph are isolated on the basis of *light*, and then each separate plate is printed with what the printer hopes is an exactly equivalent batch of printer's ink, that is, more *dyes*.

Therefore any color photograph reproduced in a book is at best an approximation of the colors in real life, an approximation that has traveled a long way from natural colors or dyes to light and then back to dyes again. The color plates in this book are as accurate as modern technology can achieve, but there still may be situations in which the piece that you have completed may not look exactly like the photograph. To paraphrase Gertrude Stein, "A red rose is *not* a red rose is *not* a red rose."

Q&A 32. Well, I'm perfectly happy with the colors of the yarns that I'm using. I'm just surprised at how the colors change as I work with them. Why does this happen?

In a way, this is similar to the situation in which you look at a 2-inch square of a "paint chip" at a paint store and decide that that's the perfect color for your living room. When that perfect color is put onto square yards and square yards of wall space, it looks anything but perfect. Especially against the sofa you just had reupholstered so expensively with its own perfect color! The only way that you can judge whether a color of anything, including yarns in a piece of braided cross-stitch, is correct, is to try it out, in order to see how it reacts in its specific environment.

Persian-type yarns have a certain "standard" color that one can judge by looking at the loosely twisted individual strands or skeins. But when one sews strands or plies of any color into stitches, the colors change slightly, depending upon the stitch structure. Two plies of light-grey Persian yarn with the same dye number will produce a slightly darker grey in braided cross-stitch, because the "lay" of the threads that form the braid casts tiny shadows over the entire surface of the stitched area.

When, as in many of the color combinations in this book, the two plies in the needle are different colors entirely, the interaction between them causes those colors to appear differently to the eye: what went into the needle eye as a grey yarn takes on a definitely pinkish cast in the finished stitch. Then that pinkish cast, in turn, interacts with the colors of the adjacent yarns. And all of these changes and interactions that result from these juxtapositions are what make color exciting.

Q&A 33. I've bought lots of colors of Persian yarn and now they are in such a jumble that I can never find a particular color whenever I need it. What's the best system for keeping the colors organized?

The system by which anybody does *anything* is the one that works best for that person. Your system of keeping spices on the spice shelf in alphabetical order (including all those spices and herbs beginning with C!) is best for you, even though your sister-in-law says that her system of keeping them in order of use is better (cinnamon, paprika, dried parsley close at hand, with cardamom, fennel, and turmeric way down at the end).

While we're at it, who says that a system is needed anyway? Some people like to rummage around with yarns in a heap. One way that

craftspeople get their inspiration, in fact, is just to notice color schemes that lie under their noses. Yarn serendipity! A jumble of yarns in which colors accidentally combine with other colors can suggest many more color schemes than you can imagine by keeping "all the blues" in one shoe box and "all the pinks" in another shoe box. It's the same situation that some quilters take advantage of: throwing several fabrics onto the floor randomly and then noticing that that print with the little pink flower looks very pretty against that solid fabric. So don't make your particular system of organizing your yarn colors so rigid that you lose the opportunity to notice unusual striking color juxtapositions.

The system that I like for keeping colors organized is one that enables me to keep the colors numerically in sequence (thus, in a somewhat orderly color sequence), in a way that shows all the colors available (instead of hiding them in boxes), but also in a way that allows me to "scramble" the colors together when I'm just "fooling around with color." My system requires the use of plastic rings 4½" in diameter. My son John used to work at a place that processes certain information by computer. Noticing that the trash heap often contained large quantities of "write rings" (plastic rings that are used somehow when "writing" on computer tapes that are being re-used, except that John's place never re-used the tapes), he wondered whether I could think of any practical use for them.

Indeed I could! Using one ring for every ten numbers in a sequence (for example, 240 through 249, or 861 through 869), I loop the cut strands of Persian yarns through the ring, and attach the identifying number by stapling on a piece of paper (I have found that Scotch tape and glue are not as sturdy.) These rings of yarn (Illus. 78) can be hung over long spikes (one spike for all yarns beginning with 2—; another for those beginning with 3—; etc.). The rings can be removed individually from the spikes and thrown around randomly on the floor while developing color schemes. If one or more strands of colors are needed, they can be removed easily from the ring without cutting the identification label. Then, when the project is completed, the rings, with the yarns still in numerical sequence, can be put back onto the spikes, where the yarns hang down

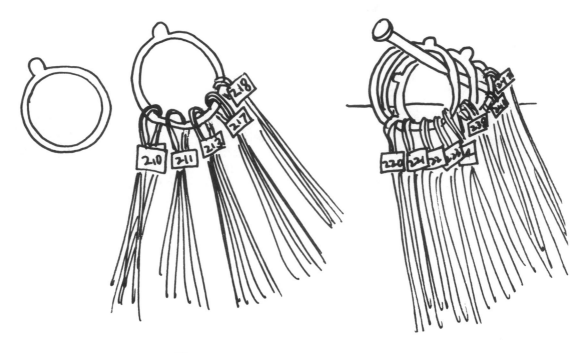

Illus. 78.

like colored Spanish moss, suggesting even more projects requiring even more tossing around of rings to select color schemes. And so it goes, far into the night! And far into the years!

If you do not have a son who can see the artistic and practical potentialities inherent in recyclable trash, you could use anything else that is annular: Metal rings that you bought to make macramé plant hangers with, but never did; cardboard doughnut-shaped rings; embroidery hoops; etc. But be advised that if you keep only ten colors on a ring, it will take a lot of rings to organize a lot of colors. If you have only a few strands of each color, you might be able to allow 20 or 30 different numbers of yarn for each ring.

Or you might be able to come up with your very own system of organizing your colors. But whatever system you use, make sure it's easy to see what you've got and, once you've seen it, know exactly what the numbers of those colors are.

But, whatever system you use for organizing and storing your yarns and your currently unfinished projects, don't make that system so neat that the things are inaccessible.

Q&A 34. Don't you think that adding embroidery stitches to a piece of braided cross-stitch takes away somewhat from its integrity? Shouldn't the piece be entirely made in one stitch?

No, I don't think that there is anything wrong with introducing an accent or two in any medium, or in any type of needlework. An occasional French knot in a counted cross-stitch piece can be very effective. So can backstitches used in combination with cross-stitch: a cross-stitched face is certainly very appealing when the features are made of backstitches, instead of having eyes and mouth made of incongruously large X's.

Similarly, an occasional backstitch or straight stitch can enhance a braided cross-stitch design. It is such infrequent embroidery stitches that I have incorporated in a few of the designs in this book. I hope that the purist won't find them too objectionable.

Q&A 35. But I don't know how to embroider at all! How do you make the straight stitch and the backstitch?

It's so easy, you'll be surprised. To make the straight stitch (Illus. 79), you simply bring the

116

yarn to the top of the canvas where you want the stitch to begin. Then, making the stitch just as long as you want, you insert the needle where you want the stitch to end, and pull the yarn to the back of the canvas. Repeat for as many straight stitches as you want. This is a very "free" stitch that can be varied at will, in direction, length, thickness of yarn, etc.

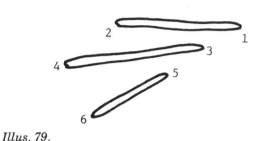

Illus. 79.

The backstitch (Illus. 80) is a more regular stitch than the straight stitch. It is usually made over the same number of threads of canvas or woven fabric, so that the stitches are all the same length. Bring your needle up to the top of canvas, the distance of one stitch away from the beginning of the row of backstitches; then go back

(hence the name of the stitch) and insert the needle down into the canvas; bring the needle up, ahead of the next backstitch, then go back to complete the second backstitch. Continue in this manner, following the contour you want to emphasize.

In counted cross-stitch (including Holbein stitch and Assisi stitch, where it is an important component), the backstitch is usually the same length as one cross-stitch (Illus. 81). The same situation prevails with braided cross-stitch. A

Illus. 81.

certain amount of care, however, must be taken when making backstitches. Because of the thick braid, backstitches that run parallel to rows of braided cross-stitch can easily "fall into the ditch"—to use a quilter's expression—if worked too tightly. Therefore, always make sure that you use a light hand, to allow the backstitches to "fluff up" and be seen easily (Illus. 82). This problem does not arise when making backstitches *across* rows of braided cross-stitches.

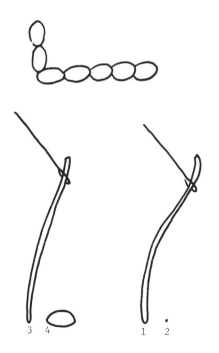

Illus. 80.

Illus. 82

Q&A 36. When stitching a completed braided cross-stitch piece to a piece of fabric—for example, when making a pillow or an eyeglass case—I can never sew on the fabric neatly. If I try to do it by sewing machine, the machine-stitching runs over some of the stitches, making those near the seam very uneven and unsightly. But if I try to sew on the piece of fabric by hand, using an overcast stitch, the hand-sewing thread looks unsightly, and often the canvas threads in the seam allowance can also be seen. Is there a better stitch I can use?

There certainly is. It is a hand-sewing stitch that gives you complete control at all times: You can see where and how to make each stitch, and the final seam is completely invisible, that is, you do not see any of the hand-sewing thread. The stitch, which is used a lot by British needleworkers, especially in toymaking, is called the "ladder stitch." It is made on the "right side" of the fabric, by making stitches alternately in the two seam allowances that have been turned to the back (Illus. 83). Knot the hand-sewing

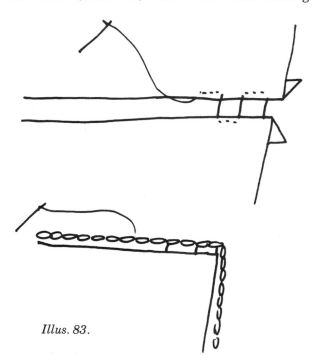

Illus. 83.

thread. Bring the needle up through one seam allowance. Insert needle in the other seam allowance, directly opposite the point where the needle

originally emerged. Then run the needle inside the second seam allowance and emerge at the spacing desired. Now insert the needle back into the first seam allowance (directly opposite the second point of emergence) and run the needle inside the first seam allowance. Continue until three or four stitches have been made. Then pull thread firmly, but not too tightly, and the seam will pull together with none of the hand-sewing thread visible. Repeat a few more stitches and pull thread again. Continue in this manner.

For braided cross-stitch work, I usually pin down the seam allowance (with pins on the outside, for easy removal), in such a way that the top row of stitches "ride the crest," that is, so that empty canvas threads do not run all the way to the very top of the seam allowance. Then I prepare the piece of fabric by folding its seam allowance to the back. I usually make the individual ladder stitches as long as *two* braided cross-stitches. Needle up through seam allowance of fabric; then across to seam allowance of braided cross-stitch piece; under two stitches, then back across to fabric; stitch of equal length in seam allowance of fabric, then back to braided cross-stitch; etc. When the ladder stitch is done properly, the stitches adjacent to the seam are not distorted in any way, and no canvas threads are visible either at the edges of the piece or at the seams.

Q&A 37. How do I block a braided cross-stitch piece after it is completed?

There's no need to block it, in the sense of dampening it, tugging at it, and pinning it into position the way one frequently has to treat a badly distorted piece of needlepoint. Braided cross-stitch never distorts the canvas. Therefore all that is necessary when it is completely worked is to lay it face-down onto a piece of thick Turkish towelling (no pinning required). Then, using a regular iron and a dampened press cloth, or a steam iron, but not applying any pressure with either kind of iron, steam the piece. Allow it to remain just where it is, without disturbing or moving it, until it is completely dry (overnight, preferably).

If the piece will be subjected to wear, as in a pillow, eyeglass case, etc., it is a good idea, as the next step, to treat it with Scotchgard® before turning the piece into the article that you are planning.

Q&A 38. How did you make the pillow from Square in a Square in a Square..., *the tote pocket from* Cat Mola, *and the* Seminole Eyeglass Case?

Before making up the article, I pressed each piece and treated it with Scotchgard® (see *Q&A 37*). I removed the masking tape from the edges of the canvas and turned down the seam allowances all around.

Each piece required a piece of backing fabric cut to allow a ½" seam allowance all around (actual size of your backing may be different from the sizes I cut, because of any variations in the type of canvas used). The backing fabric was sewn by hand onto the piece, using the ladder stitch described in *Q&A 36*.

Pillow: Sew three sides of the pillow together; insert a prepared pillow or pillow form; sew fourth side together.

Tote pocket: Sew four sides of braided cross-stitch piece and backing together. This makes an unpadded, lined pocket. Instead of making a tote bag and incorporating this pocket, I purchased a sturdy tote and hand-sewed the pocket onto one side of it.

Eyeglass case: On sides and bottom of the piece, turn down seam allowance. On top of it, turn down three rows of stitches together with seam allowance. Sew lining to piece all around, attaching the lining piece below the three rows of turned-down braided cross-stitches. Fold piece in half, to form eyeglass case. Blindstitch side and bottom together.

Q&A 39. Can braided cross-stitch pieces be made into any other kinds of articles?

Certainly! I made up only a few articles for this book, just as examples. But braided cross-stitch can be used in many other ways. There are many books available in bookstores and public libraries that describe decorative accessories, boutique items, and gifts that can be made from needlepoint or other canvas embroidery. All these articles can be made just as easily—and often more effectively—from braided cross-stitch: The completely regular appearance of it often contrasts sharply with the slightly askew appearance of blocked, reblocked, but still recalcitrant needlepoint in a made-up article.

Possible uses of a braided cross-stitch piece, other than as a picture in a frame or as one of the articles shown in this book, include:

- wall hanging (lined, unframed)—make hanging loops from canvas, and work them in a matching color of braided cross-stitches;
- footstool or piano bench cover—enlarge design to fit desired size (by adding on rows of motifs, or borders, as required);
- pin cushions (which are essentially small pillows)—work only a section of a larger design;
- table mats, dining-room table runners (seasonal or year-round), coasters;
- evening bags (clutches), purses, tote bags (braided cross-stitch piece used as an entire side, or both sides, of the tote);
- checkbook cover, telephone book cover, album cover;
- chair covers;
- and on and on.

Remember, however, to treat with Scotchgard® any article that will be subjected to wear.

Q&A 40. When plotting a possible design on graph paper, how can I know what the final size of the design will be when executed on 6.5-mesh canvas?

Refer to the table on the following page.

From Design to Graph Paper to 6.5-mesh Penelope Canvas

Height or width of design to be charted, in inches	Number of squares on graph paper with different number of *squares* per inch, and the equivalent number of *inches* that that number of stitches will cover on 6.5-mesh Penelope canvas			
	6-to-inch graph paper	*8-to-inch graph paper*	*10-to-inch graph paper*	*12-to-inch graph paper*
1	6 squares = .9″	8 squares = 1.2″	10 squares = 1.5″	12 squares = 1.8″
2	12 squares = 1.8″	16 squares = 2.5″	20 squares = 3.1″	24 squares = 3.7″
3	18 squares = 2.8″	24 squares = 3.7″	30 squares = 4.6″	36 squares = 5.5″
4	24 squares = 3.7″	32 squares = 4.9″	40 squares = 6.2″	48 squares = 7.4″
5	30 squares = 4.6″	40 squares = 6.2″	50 squares = 7.7″	60 squares = 9.2″
6	36 squares = 5.5″	48 squares = 7.4″	60 squares = 9.2″	72 squares = 11.1″
7	42 squares = 6.5″	56 squares = 8.6″	70 squares = 10.8″	84 squares = 13″
8	48 squares = 7.4″	64 squares = 9.8″	80 squares = 12.3″	96 squares = 14.8″
9	54 squares = 8.3″	72 squares = 11.1″	90 squares = 13.8″	108 squares = 16.6″
10	60 squares = 9.2″	80 squares = 12.3″	100 squares = 15.4″	120 squares = 18.5″
11	66 squares = 10.2″	88 squares = 13.5″	110 squares = 16.9″	132 squares = 20.3″
12	72 squares = 11.1″	96 squares = 14.8″	120 squares = 18.5″	144 squares = 22.2″

Formula: $\dfrac{i \cdot g}{6.5} = t,$

where i is the number of inches in height or width of the design to be charted;
g is the number of squares per inch in the graph paper used as
6.5 is the mesh-size of the Penelope canvas to be used for *tvistsöm*; and
t is the number of inches that will be covered by *tvistsöm* stitches.

EXAMPLES:

1. The design you want to render in braided cross-stitch measures 6 × 9 inches. You overlay 6-to-the-inch graph paper onto it, but you find that the grid on that paper does not accommodate the detail in your design. You overlay 8-to-the-inch graph paper and find that the design works well now. What will the finished size of your rendition be? Check the table. Height 6 inches, 8-to-the-inch graph paper, 48 squares (stitches) = 7.4″. Width 9 inches, 8-to-the-inch graph paper, 72 squares (stitches) = 11.1″. The finished size of the work will be approximately 7½ × 11 inches. You decide to do the design.

2. You have another design that you would like to render in braided cross-stitch, but it has many areas of fine detail that must be preserved in the final version. You overlay 8-to-the-inch graph paper onto the design: no good! Then 10-to-the-inch: still no good! Finally, 12-to-the-inch graph paper: it accommodates the detail well. The size of the design is 8¼ × 11¾″. What will the finished size of the braided cross-stitch on 6.5-mesh Penelope canvas be? You can't use the table, so you use the formula. Height 8.25 × 12 = 99 squares (stitches) ÷ 6.5 = 15.23″. Width 11.75 × 12 = 141 squares (stitches) ÷ 6.5 = 21.69″. The finished size will be approximately 15 × 21½ inches. You decide that that amount of work is much too much to do by your deadline (anniversary party next Thursday night). You decide to forget the idea of making a sentimental gift. Instead you'll buy some kind of biodegradable gift, perhaps a nice bottle of wine?

Q & A 41. I can figure out how to do everything in the book except how to "square-off" pictures onto graph paper—how to change curved lines into little square boxes on a grid, or how to break down a picture into all those variously colored blocks the way that television commercials sometimes do. What do you advise?

I advise you to get a copy of Gerda Bengtsson's *Danish Floral Charted Designs* (New York: Dover, 1980), which also discusses the problem.

Q&A 42. I have looked carefully through all the directions on how to make the rows of braided cross-stitches alternately from left to right and then from right to left. But nowhere in those directions do I see a word that I am sure you know: "boustrophedonically." How do you explain that glaring omission?

I was trying to hide my erudition. Did it work?

Q&A 43. Have you neglected to tell us anything else? Perhaps some personal secret of success in braided cross-stitch?

I certainly haven't deliberately left anything out. I'm not the kind of person who would give you a treasured family recipe and knowingly omit a critical ingredient. On the contrary, in my attempt to tell all and make you an avid (if not rabid) braided cross-stitch fan, I may have put you in the position of the legendary young book reviewer whose entire report was "This book told me more about penguins than I really wanted to know." If so, please forgive my enthusiasm.

Do let me know, through the book publisher, about all your successes. I would especially like to hear that this book has given you the inspiration and the knowledge to translate the scenes, images, and decorative motifs from your own life into the expressive medium of braided cross-stitches.

METRIC EQUIVALENCY CHART

MM—MILLIMETRES   CM—CENTIMETRES

INCHES TO MILLIMETRES AND CENTIMETRES

INCHES	MM	CM	INCHES	CM	INCHES	CM
⅛	3	0.3	9	22.9	30	76.2
¼	6	0.6	10	25.4	31	78.7
⅜	10	1.0	11	27.9	32	81.3
½	13	1.3	12	30.5	33	83.8
⅝	16	1.6	13	33.0	34	86.4
¾	19	1.9	14	35.6	35	88.9
⅞	22	2.2	15	38.1	36	91.4
1	25	2.5	16	40.6	37	94.0
1¼	32	3.2	17	43.2	38	96.5
1½	38	3.8	18	45.7	39	99.1
1¾	44	4.4	19	48.3	40	101.6
2	51	5.1	20	50.8	41	104.1
2½	64	6.4	21	53.3	42	106.7
3	76	7.6	22	55.9	43	109.2
3½	89	8.9	23	58.4	44	111.8
4	102	10.2	24	61.0	45	114.3
4½	114	11.4	25	63.5	46	116.8
5	127	12.7	26	66.0	47	119.4
6	152	15.2	27	68.6	48	121.9
7	178	17.8	28	71.1	49	124.5
8	203	20.3	29	73.7	50	127.0

YARDS TO METRES

YARDS	METRES	YARDS	METRES	YARDS	METRES	YARDS	METRES	YARDS	METRES
⅛	0.11	2⅛	1.94	4⅛	3.77	6⅛	5.60	8⅛	7.43
¼	0.23	2¼	2.06	4¼	3.89	6¼	5.72	8¼	7.54
⅜	0.34	2⅜	2.17	4⅜	4.00	6⅜	5.83	8⅜	7.66
½	0.46	2½	2.29	4½	4.11	6½	5.94	8½	7.77
⅝	0.57	2⅝	2.40	4⅝	4.23	6⅝	6.06	8⅝	7.89
¾	0.69	2¾	2.51	4¾	4.34	6¾	6.17	8¾	8.00
⅞	0.80	2⅞	2.63	4⅞	4.46	6⅞	6.29	8⅞	8.12
1	0.91	3	2.74	5	4.57	7	6.40	9	8.23
1⅛	1.03	3⅛	2.86	5⅛	4.69	7⅛	6.52	9⅛	8.34
1¼	1.14	3¼	2.97	5¼	4.80	7¼	6.63	9¼	8.46
1⅜	1.26	3⅜	3.09	5⅜	4.91	7⅜	6.74	9⅜	8.57
1½	1.37	3½	3.20	5½	5.03	7½	6.86	9½	8.69
1⅝	1.49	3⅝	3.31	5⅝	5.14	7⅝	6.97	9⅝	8.80
1¾	1.60	3¾	3.43	5¾	5.26	7¾	7.09	9¾	8.92
1⅞	1.71	3⅞	3.54	5⅞	5.37	7⅞	7.20	9⅞	9.03
2	1.83	4	3.66	6	5.49	8	7.32	10	9.14

Index